THREE COMEDIES AND A TRAGEDY

BY

ED WODE

Copyright © 2007
By Ed Wode

Published by Horned Toad Productions, Inc.
Long Beach, Ca. 90810
edwode@gmail.com
Distributed by
www.lulu.com and HTP, Inc
Copyright © 2007
By Ed Wode
ISBN: 978-0-6151-4157-2
Creative Common Attribution
Non-commercial Share Alike 2.0

4

TABLE OF CONTENTS

Divine Retribution, the Trail of Edger Most .... page 5 to 108

Reverend Money .... page 109 to 190

The Demagogues .... page 191 to 332

Marshall's Agency .... page 333 to 377

DIVINE RETRIBUTION, THE TRIAL OF EDGER MOST

A COMEDY

BY

ED WODE

© 2006 by Ed Wode
edwode@gmail.com

DIVINE RETRIBUTION, the TRIAL OF EDGER MOST

MAIN CHARACTERS

EDGER MOST, JR – He is one of the world's richest men, a multi-billionaire conservationist philanthropist who donates huge sums to charities, especially those to save endangered species. He is also one of the world's biggest hypocrites as he hunts these same animals and kills them for trophies. He is the clone offspring of Edger Most, Sr.

EDNA MOST – She is the Edger Most Sr.'s transgender clone daughter and the sister-lover of Edger Most.

JUDGE S. DREAD SIMBA – a wiry leonine judge with an eye for the ladies. He presides over the trial of the century, the trial for murder of Edger Most.

JOHNIE COCK – defense attorney for Edger Most. Paid a million dollars a day to represent Edger Most, but would rather not as he doesn't think he can win.

MR. GREENWAY – Privatized prosecutor of Edger Most who prosecutes Edger Most for murdering the endangered Argali Ram, a capital offense in the times depicted.

SCOUTMASTER BATER – A child molester who testifies for the prosecution against Edger Most to save his bacon.

HOLINESS DELI TEK – a Dalai Lama type of religious leader who has survived being ejected from his country thanks to the largess of the C.I.A. As leader of Argalianity, he worships the trinity of Edger Most, the Argali Ram, and the Holy Ghost.

THE ARGALI RAM – This is the world's largest sheep with spiral horns measuring 56 inches. He is considered to be a living God by the natives, but an endangered animal by conservationists.

MR. BIRD – Teenage Boy Scout and defense witness against Scoutmaster Bater's testimony for the prosecution.

Two gay Bailiffs, Osama bin Laden, a fellow terrorist, natives and miscellaneous jurors.

DIVINE RETRIBUTION, THE TRIAL OF EDGER MOST

SETTING: Remote highlands in Central Asia.

AT RISE: An ARGALI ram adorned with a burdensome rack of horns resembling a six foot coiled snake is sitting next to a boulder resting his head against his hoof much in the manner of Auguste Rodin's sculpture "The Thinker." He is an animal of a protected endangered species. As sheep don't normally talk, this part will be played by an actor dressed as the ram.

                ARGALI RAM
Wow! Another hot day! Seems like the world is getting hotter by the year. Better think about moving up the slope as soon as I get my breath. Must be at least 40 or 50 degrees, a real scorcher! Maybe I better get a haircut like those tame sheep, but I can't stand those two legged hornless barbers who jabber jabber jabber like monkeys. They grow ugly beards and stink like goats too. Mum. The grass looks tasty here, but not plentiful. There's always some trade off if you want to eat. Speaking of eating, I better keep a sharp weather eye out for Simba. He likes to eat too. And I'm one of his favorite meals. Gosh! I wonder what's going on. It's surprisingly deserted here today for such a fine day. Maybe there's more food on the next mountain. Worst luck. These horns are too heavy to schlep over there this time of day. I better stay here, have a snack and head up the slope. I'll move in the morning.

Suddenly a shot rings out and the ram is hit and falls dead.

CURTAIN DOWN/CURTAIN UP

EDGER MOST is triumphantly posed with his foot on the dead ARGALI while his picture is being taken with the help of an OSAMA BIN LADEN look alike. There is also one taken together. This picture of the two together later appears in Taxidermy Museum Magazine and is used in EDGER'S TRIAL.

> EDGER MOST
> Well, it cost me twenty million to get this trophy, but it has been worth every penny. More bang for the buck than a space ride anytime. And the publicity will be outrageous. Wait till they see this rack of horns at the Safari Club. Maybe they'll give me a gold ring without having to make all 300 kills. Fat chance! It's a chore, but one I am prepared to endure until I get one of those most rare rings. I dearly love public service. The Smythsonium Museum has already named their Hall of Mammals after me for my conservation efforts. Not to mention a few million donation, of course! Impressed the Interior Dept. Fish and Wildlife Service too; that's for sure. They give me all the exemptions I want to kill rare animals. Me and my fellow millionaires keep them so busy handing out exemptions, they hardly have time for anything else. Rare animal species friends, just like national forests, need pruning to keep the species healthy and who is in a better position to do this properly than millionaires? Of course we leave the forests to the lumber companies we own. It's another example of privatization saving taxpayers a ton of money. Let's have a toast to privatization. (Pops Champaign and drinks from bottle.) Sir, would you take my picture? Thank you for taking my picture. How about one together for the folks back home?

> OSAMA
> Glad to oblige a fellow hunter.

As the two are posing together, there is a scurry of natives wearing animal masks that attack EDGER and drag him away. OSAMA stands there smiling as EDGER is dragged away. He whispers confidentially to a confederate.

                    OSAMA
Now, we'll see what this fool has to say for himself. Too bad he's not ours to make talk.

EDGER MOST has been arrested and is now on trial. His captors are worshippers of ARGALI sheep. They are masked as various animals. The murdered sheep was considered to be one of their Gods.

                    JUDGE SIMBA
(A mountain lion masked native.)
EDGER MOST, you are accused of murdering this ARGALI God because you coveted his wonderful rack of horns for your rare animal trophy room.

                    EDGER
I didn't know this was an Argali god. I thought he was a garden-variety wild sheep hereabouts; a MARCO POLO or a BLUEBEARD. Besides, I paid twenty million to shoot this animal. You would kill him and eat him without paying a cent. How can you judge me an avowed conservationist?

                    JUDGE
You mean avowed hypocrite EDGER MOST. That's wrong in TAZTIKISTAN even if it's the main religion in America. You had no right to pay money to kill this ARGALI either. He is part of my food chain provided by God. I have every right to kill him and eat him. You none.

                    EDGER
What about my food chain? Aren't I allowed one?

                    JUDGE
Yours is at the supermarket.

                    EDGER
I want representation. I want JOHNNY COCK. I can afford the best.

JUDGE
We don't pay attorneys in TAZTIKISTAN, so you'll have to settle for a court appointed attorney. This wild ass will most appropriately be your defense attorney.

EDGER
I protest. I don't want no ass for an attorney if I'm on trial for my life.

JUDGE
Maybe you'd rather have this vulture?

EDGER
Yes give me a vulture for a defense attorney. At least they are carrion eaters like the real McCoy.

JUDGE
How do you plead EDGER MOST?

VULTURE
He pleads guilty your royal honor Judge Simba.

EDGER
Now just a minute, I've heard of hungry vultures, I mean lawyers, but you take the cake. Don't I get any say? I'm innocent.

JUDGE
None is necessary. I find you guilty of murder in the first degree and sentence you to be staked out on an ant hill Indian style until you beg to be eaten alive by your lawyer and his relatives.

EDGER
Can't I have a jury trial?

JUDGE
No one else has ever stooped as low as you, so you have no peers. No peers, no jury trial. Take him away and give the ants a taste.

EDGER
Isn't there something I can do to make restitution?

JUDGE
Admit you are a spy for the C.I.A.

EDGER
I haven't worked for them in years. I swear to you on my Boy Scout honor.

JUDGE
In that case, skip the ants... (Beat)

EDGER
Praise be to Allah, the all-merciful one.

JUDGE
Skewer and barbecue him Cajon style instead. I'm really famished and I get the first bite.

Edger is led away begging for his life and made to bend over. A large stake is pressed against his rectum. Edger screams for mercy as there is a:

DOWN CURTAIN/ UP CURTAIN:

Edger's is at home back safely in the United States. He is slumped in a chair asleep. He wakes screaming from a terrible recurring bad dream about the above events.

EDGER
Phew! A nightmare about that trial again! It was so real and so horrible; I still can't believe I'm alive.

(There is a loud knock at the door)

EDGER
Now who in Sam Hill is that? I'm not expecting anyone.

(Another loud knock)

> **EDGER**
> O.K., O.K.! I'm coming. The butler would be off today.

(Opens the door)

There are two husky marshals standing there. (Bailiffs when court is in session)

> **MARSHALL**
> Are you EDGER MOST?

> **EDGER**
> Yes officer. What's wrong? I bought a whole book of policemen's power ball tickets already and gave them to my butler. Don't tell me he won. He won't want to work anymore.

> **MARSHALL**
> EDGER MOST, you are under arrest for violating the Endangered Species Act by murdering a God. The people of TAZTIKISTAN are wild ARGALI sheep God worshippers.

> **EDGER**
> You mean sheep buggerers don't you? I know I killed that endangered Argali, but isn't it a bit of a stretch to term an animal a God. That's been a verboten practice since the Old Testament days. Besides I donated twenty million to the endangered species wing of the Taxidermy Museum of America and got to use one of their exemptions to kill rare animals.

> **MARSHALL**
> That doesn't give you the right to commit Godicide without a license. God is a very rare animal.

EDGER
I gave a ten million donation to those animal worshipper natives of that godforsaken place for killing their Argali. Now they can afford to build a church and start a real religion. Who worships animals anymore anyway? Maybe a few Hindus! Could be a billion Philistines for all I care. Rag head retards whatever.

MARSHALL
You killed their God. Have you no shame?

EDGER
Who the hell are you to judge me?

MARSHALL
I'm the man dummy. Put your hands behind you unless you want to commit suicide. I have the authority to hunt and kill you mister and they pay me good money to do it.

EDGER
What's the world coming to when billionaires get treated like white trash or black garbage?

MARSHALL
When justice calls, it's your ass even if you're the richest man in the world.

EDGER
You must get your anal tips from Google's Planet Bathhouse back window spy cam.

MARSHALL
Let's go buddy. This ain't Comedy Central.

CURTAIN DOWN/CURTAIN UP

Edger is sitting in a jail holding room talking to his lawyer JOHNNY COCK. He should have a team similar to the O.J. Simpson dream team. As an economy, the team can be just JOHNNY COCK. COCK is the highest paid attorney in the world at one million per day.

JOHNNY COCK
I think your best bet is to plead not guilty to laying in wait to commit premeditated murder. Say it was an accident. You were just trying to protect the Argali from terrorists and your gun accidentally discharged. I hear some were in the area hunting.

EDGER
But Mr. Cock! He's stuffed, mounted, and displayed in my trophy room. I've been made an honorary member of every major hunting organization in the world, even www.datingcannibals.com.

JOHNNY
You meant to say chapel instead of trophy room, didn't you Mr. Most?

EDGER
Well, yes. Of course! I had him stuffed and mounted as an object of veneration, like the Russian icons I collect to decorate my chapel.

JOHNNY
Almost perfect! We can work on that card. It makes me nostalgic for the good ole days when if you were clergy you could get away with anything. It was almost as good as the race card.

EDGER
I can use that too.

JOHNNY
But you're white.

EDGER
Not really. I'm three quarters black Irish.

JOHNNY
Now we're getting somewhere. No, I take that back. I don't think black Irish counts for much. In fact black Irish have about as much chance of

playing the race card as they do of drawing a royal flush in the toilet. Black hair, brown eyes and dark skin doth not a raven make. A crow by any other name is still a crow quoth Edger Allen Poe.

EDGER
This is unjust. It's discrimination against my racial preference. It's illegal to discriminate.

JOHNNY
Discrimination is not illegal. Only some discrimination! Homosexual scout leaders, territorial dogs, white males who have been passed over because of affirmative action and people of middle Eastern background who want to learn to fly planes that don't have to land or take off are all fair game for discrimination. And it's open season all the time on former felons that supposedly have paid for their crimes. They are permanently deprived of their civil rights, unless they can afford to buy a presidential pardon.

EDGER
But, discrimination against white males! Surely you're kidding Mr. Cock?

JOHNNY
Let's drop the formalities Mr. Most. I'm Johnny and you're Edger. O.K!

EDGER
Most assuredly Mr. Cock, I mean Johnny.

JOHNNY
Now then Edger! Didn't I get a guy off who was a double lock for the death penalty? Isn't that why you hired me? Do I seem like a kidder to you?

EDGER
White males? What kind of a country is this Johnny?

JOHNNY
A very discriminating country.

EDGER
What we need is another Martin Luther Queen.

JOHNNY
It was King EDGER. Anyway, now that you have your story straight, we'll see you in court tomorrow.

CURTAIN DOWN/CURTAIN UP

EDGER and JOHNNY are in a courtroom waiting for the judge to enter. This can either be a jury trial, a tribunal or judge only. The privatized prosecutor MR. GREENWAY is present along with the rest of the denizens that inhabit a court in session.

The judge enters and the bailiff announces that everyone should rise. The judge looks suspiciously like Simba from the dream sequence. He has the leonine look without the mask.

EDGER
This is a kangaroo court. That's the same hanging judge from my dream about what happened when the natives arrested me for killing the ARGALI, sans his lion mask.

JOHNNY
Careful! That's the real JUDGE DREAD.

EDGER
And I dread him; believe me. He's already sentenced me to be eaten alive by vultures.

JOHNNY
Are you referring to my fellow members of the bar?

EDGER
No pseudos, I mean real honest to god vultures.

JOHNNY
O.K! So we're pseudo, so what? Everything else is pseudo. We eat genetically altered pseudo food pumped full of female hormones that turn us into pseudo males that vote for pseudo representatives, who pass pseudo laws, that govern a pseudo democracy for the profit of pseudo capitalist corporations that are really communist countries in disguise. Pseudo may soon be privatized and made America's official religion.

EDGER
And public opinion polls, by a margin of two to one are against almost every pseudo law that is passed. Should politicians take such polls seriously?

JOHNNY
No! Polls be damned. Politicians know what is best for America. The public is a bud-brained besotted mob that deserves more sports on TV.

EDGER
Are you suggesting that politicians may really be in touch with reality and that polls reflect a kind of alcohol brain damage of the public?

JOHNNY
Only minimally in both cases! I have the greatest respect for Joe Six-pack and Mary Bimbat who are the backbone of America even if their brains have been shrunk down to birdbrain size by the great American media dumb down machine. Anybody that would believe that Budweiser crap is the king of beers would believe the Taj Mahal is a marshmallow and try roasting it. Of course now that we have overlapping sporting events that never end, there is no time to do anything else but drink Bud and piss. The same dumb fucking Bud brains who buy Bud because it spends the most

money claiming to be the king of beers vote for the biggest dumb liar for president because he spends the most money on TV ads. Then they are shocked to hear he lies and cheats and is dumb as a stone just like them. You're right I don't have much respect for Joe and Mary because they are giving dumb a bad name. This couple I know…

CURTAIN DOWN/CURTAIN UP

Bedroom stage area in a house or apartment:

DUDE SIXPAC and MARY BIMBAT are watching a sporting event on a large TV. They are drinking a lot of Bud and cheering the home team.

DUDE
Another one for the home team! That's the fiftieth point for Osama the eightieth time this year. This guy reminds me of Michael Jordan except he's almost white.

MARY
He's an Arab.

DUDE
He's seven-six. They don't make Arabs that big.

MARY
The Osama was six-six.

DUDE
What do you mean was? Last week in his latest video, he threatened to blow up Staples Center with Jack Nicholson in it.

MARY
The President thinks he may be dead.

DUDE
Wait until after the election. That guy is about as dead as my dick on a double dose of Viagra.

MARY
Who you voting for to be president DUDE?

DUDE
The guy who drinks the most Bud of course!

MARY
I hear Bud is used to wean rich babies from the hard stuff.

DUDE
Cool…

MARY
I don't know. That super bowl ad, "cradle to grave with Buds" is stretching a little.

DUDE
Gotta get started someplace! Besides that ad was for marijuana. Get me another Bud sweet buns!

MARY
And more popcorn baby cakes?

DUDE
Yeah. And bring the strap on soccer balls too.

CURTAIN DOWN/CURTAIN UP

EDGER AND MR. COCK are still having a talk while waiting for court to begin.

MR. COCK

There's what sports addition leads too. Kinky sex.

EDGER
Get me out of here. I don't care if it costs me a couple hundred million.

MR. COCK
If there's a bail bondsmen with enough funds... There's never been a bail this high.

EDGER
Why are they picking on me? This Endangered Species law was not supposed to effect billionaires. I spent a fortune getting my version passed that protects Right Brained Snail Darters and Left Footed Praying Mantises. I'm one of the world's leading conservationists myself.

MR. COCK
Its pressure groups like the Elders of Zion who have no respect for big money.

EDGER
Who the hell are they. They're a myth aren't they?

MR. COCK
No way. They hired me once to sue a holocaust denier.

EDGER
Did you win?

MR. COCK
You bet. I've never lost a case.

EDGER
That's why I hired you. But what do the Elders of Zion have to do with me?

MR. COCK
They think global warming is another holocaust plot to kill Jews.

EDGER
What's that have to do with me?

MR. COCK
They don't like goy billionaires.

EDGER
What do they plan to do?

MR. COCK
The rumor is…

CURTAIN DOWN/CURTAIN UP

A gathering of the ELDER OF ZION is meeting to decide the fate of the world. They vote to make EDGER MOST a human sacrifice in order to placate the global warming gods. They get no respect however, because they can't remember his name or their own for that matter. They are almost senile old people!

MANFRIED EDSELWEISSER
Ve don't get no respect Arnold Rosenvelt.

ARNOLD ROSENVELT
Yes, Manfried Edselweisser,
ve don't get no respect.

HELGA MEGAWART
Ve don't get no damn respect.

MANFRIED
Vatch your filthy mouth Helga Megavart!

HELGA
Shut your face Pretzelwiser. My name is Megawart, not Megavart!

MANFRIED
You could 'a fooled me.

ARNOLD
Enough already! You sound like a bunch of Bud Goys. No vonder ve don't get no respect.

MANFRIED
Yes we don't get no respect anyway.

HELGA
How can we decide the fate of the world if we don't get no respect?

ARNOLD
We'll decide it respect or not.

MANFRIED
Right we'll decide it anyway.

HELGA
I'm witch you. How about we pray to god for an end to global warming?

ARNOLD
We should have tried that before the holocaust.

MANFRIED
What else can you do?

HELGA
How about a human sacrifice? It worked for Abraham.

ARNOLD
Mozel Tov! The Aztecs had a lot of success with it too until Columbus toasted them.

HELGA
Yeah, the Catholics had their own Christian version called Auto de Fes.

ARNOLD
Fes? Were they sacrificing homos?

HELGA
No dummy, Jews

ARNOLD
It's got to be a goy this time. Jews are bad luck.

MANFRIED
But, who!

HELGA
I know. That sneaky billionaire hypocrite who kills endangered big horned sheep! He's a goy too.

ARNOLD
If he's a goy, how'd he get to be a billionaire?

MANFRIED
Some of them get lucky.

ARNOLD
What's his name?

MANFRIED
Edsel. No that's my name!

ARNOLD
I got it... toast.

HELGA
Close dummy, it's Most, something Most!

ARNOLD
That's it Edsel Most.

HELGA
It's not a women dummy.

MANFRIED
I am not a women you filthy mouth.

HELGA
Then what are you little prick?

ARNOLD
He's an old neuter goat like you.

They all start improv talking at the same time and finally agree.

ALL THREE
EDGER! It's EDGER MOST.

They begin dancing around like witches brewing a curse on Edger Most. They chant "Edger Most, Edger Most, You are toast, you are toast." Repeat.

CURTAIN DOWN/CURTAIN UP

The trial of EDGER MOST has begun. The prosecutor is ready to make his opening statement. JUDGE H. DREAD SIMBA is presiding. The judge should be of a likeable even comical demeanor. He should not be of the stern type, although he can fake it when appropriate

>JUDGE SIMBA
>MR.GREENWAY, is the prosecution ready to proceed with its opening argument?

>PROSECUTOR
>I am your honor. Ladies and gentlemen of the jury, the state is going to prove to you beyond a reasonable doubt that EDGER MOST, the accused sitting here before you, is guilty of the heinous crime of Godicide, a homeland security capital offense clause added recently to the Endangered Species Act by the president. Not only did he kill a rare God, he did it in the sneakiest of ways. He hid in the brush and waited until the ARGALI was deep in thought. Then, he rudely interrupted the divine beast's meditation by crashing a bullet like a cymbal blast from hell straight into his brain. The state proscribes this kind of laying in wait ambush and defines it as a special circumstance crime punishable by death. What is most heinously inexcusable is that MR.MOST not only killed a beast on the endangered species list; he killed a rare divine thought in progress. This is a capital crime equivalent to using discarded human embryos as oyster shooters in a shot of Tequila. In the information age, even common thoughts by common people are a precious commodity, especially when needed by pols for polls, as in

public opinion polls: not to be confused with the Poles that used to be the butt of Polish jokes. Polish joke Poles are part of NATO now and deserve not to be confused with public opinion polls or maypoles. That's no polish joke folks! Divine thoughts by divine souls are our most precious commodity. Anybody that interrupts one in the rude fashion that Edger Most interrupted the ARGALI'S should die just as rudely with a bullet in the back of the head Chinese style. Lethal injection is too good for the likes of Godicides and should be reserved for cats and dogs and pidgins. This defendant shows no respect for the law either civilized or uncivilized and must be punished accordingly. We will show this jury beyond a reasonable doubt why this man is guilty of murder one, both literally and figuratively. He is also suspected of the really serious crime of pirating billions of copies of Microsoft's Windows OS and selling them for half price to headhunters and terrorists in the third world. Because of this, BILL GATES standing on the Forbes richest list has been adversely affected and he is furious. His lobbying effort to have a new law passed making software piracy a capital crime is expected to pass congress as soon as he settles his current monopoly dispute with the government. Fairly for monopolists of course. He wants EDGER MOST to be toast and so does the state. Thank you members of this court and thanks your honor for allowing private enterprise to do the job in this court that hitherto has been botched by those on the public dole who have been posing as prosecutors

JUDGE SIMBA

My sentiments exactly! Woops, just kidding. Strike that from the record. MR.GREENWAY is a privatized prosecutor. For the benefit of public enlightenment about how this evolutionary judicial process works, would you please explain it MR. GREENWAY? I'm not sure I understand myself.

MR. GREENWAY

Most certainly JUDGE SIMBA! The bench wants the public to be aware that this prosecution is an example of the way that privatization works in the Orange County California justice system to save taxpayers precious dollars. Prosecutors are guns for hire in the true tradition of the old West and go from courthouse to courthouse peddling their services just like real peddlers. Why hire a third rate hack full time when you can get the services of a ruthless genius part time for less money. And it's much fairer to the defendant, because we don't make bumpily mistakes like hiding evidence that can later be found. Privatizing prosecution guarantees successful prosecution in this case or I will donate my fee to a worthy charity such as the Buena Park Southern Baptist Homeless Shelter. I just hope my infamous opponent, the criminal defense attorney MR.COCK, will make the same gesture.

JUDGE SIMBA

Thank you MR. GREENWAY! Would you care to respond MR. COCK?

MR. COCK

Win or lose, I'll donate my fee to the same worthy cause MR.GREENWAY. By the way GREENWAY, did you say you were a part time hack and full time genius or a full time hack and part time genius?

There is a gasp of delight from the gallery as JOHNNY takes a bow.

JUDGE SIMBA

Order, order in the court. No more outbursts or I'll empty the gallery. Thank you for the privatization plug MR.GREENWAY. Everyone should know what a great job private enterprise is doing to save the taxpayer from prodigal bureaucrats. Let me, however, admonish the jury that we are not here to promote privatization at the expense of justice just to save the taxpayer money. That would be judicial prostitution. And MR. GREENWAY, have you forgotten that I was presiding several years ago when you prosecuted that illegal So Baptist Homeless Shelter for operating without a license and caused it to be closed? And I'm sure MR. COCK is aware of this too. Lawyer's tricks! If I wasn't one myself, I'd say get rid of them all. MR.COCK, are you ready to make your opening speech?

MR. COCK

I am your honor. Ladies and Gentleman of the court, honorable JUDGE SIMBA, all people everywhere concerned with the survival of religious freedom and the restoration of the racial place in the sun of the black Irish, I am going to prove the innocence of EDGER MOST, pardon the pun, in a *MOST* controversial way. Why will it be so controversial? It will be so, because by telling the truth, the whole truth and nothing but the truth, we will shake this country right off its foundation of watered down and unconstitutional laws. Of course the truth norm used will be based on the standard employed by major political figures. This, of course, is to define the truth as mostly a pack of lies. If this rule is the truth, as everyone knows it is, why are political figures seldom required to explain their rhetorical peccadilloes? Why? Because, conventional wisdom holds that an erroneous opinion is not to be considered a deceit as long as it is pleasingly disguised as the truth. Therefore, the most deceitfully presented opinion is most often considered to be the truth if it is what is pleasant to hear. I will therefore try to win your good opinion by being more pleasant than the prosecutor. In spite of the sociopathic talent that is required of a prosecutor in order to be able to enjoy sending guilty and innocent alike to the gallows without so much as a pang of conscience, I am sure MR. GREENWAY is a pleasantly well-meaning citizen. I will pleasantly as possible show you how the unpleasant task of killing rare animals is a necessary adjunct if America is to be an example of a true market economy. One could look at it as the necessary first step to privatizing hunting and fishing, even before social security. Even though that stupid issue has all but disappeared from radar screens since the collapse of the stock market, plunder will recycle itself as surely as the stock market. And last but not least I will show you how the defendant has a genetic and religious right to kill rare animals in spite of discriminatory laws against billionaires and black Irish. Thank you.

JUDGE SIMBA
A most unusual opening speech MR. COCK! If this is an example of your pleasant aspect sir, let me warn you in advance that contempt of court is my middle name.

EDGER MOST
(A stage whisper to Johnny)
Gee, I thought it was DREAD.

JOHNNY
It is you damned fool.

JUDGE SIMBA
Side bar Gentleman.

The lawyers go to the side bar

JUDGE SIMBA
No more stage whispers from your client that everyone can hear MR. COCK. Your client is not

an actor even though I know that's your specialty. And MR. GREENWAY, no recriminations against MR. COCK for his accurately insulting remarks toward you. Serve you right for your over-the-top bragging. And both of you, no more legal pranks at my expense or it will be at your expense the next time. How many witnesses do you plan to have MR. GREENWAY

MR. GREENWAY
Just one your honor! The spiritual leader of Tastikistan, THE DELI TIK.

JUDGE SIMBA
And you MR. COCK?

MR. COCK
Just one your honor, the same one as the prosecution!

MR. COCK
Good. This should be simple to decide with one witness.

MR. COCK
I also plan to put my client on the stand.

MR. GREENWAY
Wonderful news! Shall we warm up the chair MR.COCK?

MR. COCK
Yes, for when Orange County nationalizes prosecution and you become a hack defense attorney. (The Judge chortles)

CURTAIN DOWN/CURTAINUP

The trial continues after the DELI TIK is sworn in as a witness of the prosecution and questioned by MR. GREENWAY. MR. COCK then crosses him. He then becomes a witness for the defense. MR. COCK questions him and MR. GREENWAY crosses him. This may require taking poetic liberties with the norm trial process.

                        JUDGE SIMBA
Please give your full name and address and swear to tell the truth according to your religion.

                        DELI TIK
My name is my title, THE DELI TIK: (spells) address the TAZTIKISTAN MOST MONASTERY, TAZTIKISTAN. (Spells) I swear to tell the truth according to the one true religion ARGAIANITY. (He kisses an object hanging around his neck)

                        JUDGE SIMBA
What is the object you kissed?

                        DELI
A crucifix!

                        JUDGE SIMBA
But that symbol is already taken.

                        DELI
This one has EDGER MOST on it.

                        JUDGE
But he is not a martyr yet.

                        DELI
His lawyer has assured us he will be soon.

                        JUDGE
You didn't hear that jurors! That's privileged information. Strike that from the record. We don't want to have a mistrial.

                        DELI
Quite true your honor. We don't want to disappoint 5 million worshippers in Taztikistan and quite a few thousand in California.

JUDGE

That goes without saying but I think you're jumping the gun slightly. This trial is not over yet and you are presumed innocent until found guilty in America. Besides, I think putting your Argali sheep God on it would be more authentic.

DELI

We thought of that, but animal worship is a bit too much like idol worship. And that's not Christian

JUDGE

I fail to see much difference. Praying to an image of EDGER MOST is still idol worship.

DELI

He is not a Madonna, an Elvis, or a Michael Jackson.

JUDGE

Let's hope not. Your witness MR.GREENWAY!

MR. GREENWAY

Thank you your honor. How does one address you MR. DELI TIK?

DELI TIK

Holiness is OK.

MR. GREENWAY

Would you please explain your title The Deli Tik, Holiness and tell us a little about your religion Argalianity?

DELI TIK

By all means! I am The Deli Tik of Taztikistan. That would be a position similar to chief Ayatollah of Iran, the Dalai Lama of Tibet or what that phony Pat Robertson thinks he is. My country has recently been freed from the scourge of communism and is once more a theocracy. This means I am both the spiritual and political leader of my country. Our religion Argalianity is a fusion of Argali sheep worship and Christianity.

MR. GREENWAY
When did this fusion come about Holiness?

DELI TIK
When SAINT EDGER donated ten million to renovate our several thousand-year old Most Monastery!

MR. GREENWAY
Why is it called Most Monastery?

DELI TIK
Same as Staples Center in L.A. EDGER MOST paid for it.

MR. GREENWAY
Where does the Christianity come in?

DELI TIK
Everything same except we worship EDGER MOST instead of JESUS. Same as Moonies worship Reverend Moon as the new messiah.

MR. GREENWAY
Yes but Jesus appointed Moon his successor messiah I'm told.

DELI TIK
Moon's been fired. On a hillside in Taztikistan on June 30 Y2K, Jesus came to Edger Most and told him he was going to be the new messiah because Moon resigned in a pique when he was sent to jail for tax evasion which he blamed on his accountants overzealous worship. This has been proven to be true.

MR. GREENWAY
And you believe this Holiness?

DELI TIK
I read it in the Moonies Washington Times newspaper when I was working for the CIA so it must be true.

MR. GREENWAY
Have you got turnip trucks in Taztikistan Holiness?

DELI TIK
Yes, but I didn't fall off one on my Holy head.

MR. GREENWAY
Are you sure? If Edger Most is a messiah, I am the Holy Ghost.

DELI TIK
You are the Holy Ghost? You were demoted by the Catholics weren't you? Glad to meet you anyway. Maybe you'd like to become a convert. Then we'd have a trinity just like Christianity. What an unbeatable combination. The Sheep, the Most and the Holy Ghost! Has a ring of truth to it too. What do you say?

MR. GREENWAY
I'll pass for now. I don't think my bank account would meet your criteria for Gods.

DELI TEK
I think all religions could use a new messiah with big bucks. It's time to put religious competition to rest and practice genuine ecumenicalism. There are plenty of bucks to be raked in by everybody without resorting to killing the competition.

MR. GREENWAY
That's all the questions the state has your honor.

JUDGE SIMBA
Mr. Cock. He's now the defense's witness to cross.

MR. COCK
Your Holiness, you were just kidding now when you offered to make MR. GREENWAY part of your trinity weren't you?

DELI TEK
Not really. Trinities have been proven to increase market share by a magnitude of ten.

MR. COCK
That's it for my cross.

JUDGE SIMBA
Your witness then!

MR. COCK
Don't we have to swear him in again as my witness?

JUDGE SIMBA
To SATAN with swearing in! The whole testimony is a pack of lies. You're still under oath your HOLY DELI or whatever.

MR. COCK
Your Holiness, you've known Mr. Most for a long time, haven't you?

DELI TIK
Yes, since we were both employees of the CIA.

MR. COCK
Has he ever done anything to your knowledge that would disqualify him from being a messiah?

DELI TEK
No.

MR. COCK
That's all the questions I have your honor.

JUDGE SIMBA
MR. GREENWAY. Re-Cross?

MR. GREENWAY
Yes your honor. I certainly do. (Very sarcastic) Your holiness, does murdering your god qualify Mr. Most to be your messiah?

DELI TIK
Yes.

MR.GREENWAY
Can you explain how?

DELI TEK
To kill a God, you must be a greater God.

MR. GREENWAY
I have no more questions for this witness your honor.

JUDGE SIMBA
Are you changing your plea to guilty MR. COCK?

MR COCK
No your honor. While there's jury nullification, there's still hope.

JUDGE SIMBA
No speeches MR.COCK. Is your witness ready?

JOHNNY
He is your honor.

EDGER MOST is put on the stand in his own defense, an unusual move. Defense attorneys usually try to avoid putting their clients on the stand no matter that they are guilty or innocent. This does not in imply guilt or innocence in any way. It reflects a fear that the defendant will inadvertently incriminate himself when examined. A very small mistake in testimony can be blow up to make it seem there is guilt when there is none. This is another bold move by JOHNNY COCK. The judge swears in EDGER MOST who has converted to ARGALIANITY.

JUDGE SIMBA
What is your religion MR. MOST?

EDGER
Argalianity, your honor.

JUDGE SIMBA
And do your swear to tell the truth so help you God on this mockery of a religion?

EDGER
I do your honor.

JUDGE SIMBA
Your witness MR. COCK

JOHNNY
(Examining Edger)
Now then, MR. MOST, what made you think you had the right to kill an animal on the Endangered Species Act protected list?

EDGER
Many things! First off, all living things are fair game to be killed for food if they become part of somebody's food chain. The Argali is part of the food chain of the people of Taztikistan where I have become a citizen. Secondly, the law in regard to protection of animals is watered down to the point of being worthless like most laws passed by the American congress since the halcyon days of the New Deal. Made so purposely by lawmakers who intend that it be possible for special interests to circumvent them! These special interests are usually large campaign contributors that expect to profit unfairly by their bought influence. Thirdly, as a member of the black race, I should be allowed to catch up on what the white man has been doing since time immemorial… killing for the sport of it. We blacks are number one in women's tennis, golf, track, basketball and other sports. Why not

big game hunting? To deny us this remedial indulgence would be anti-affirmative action gross racial discrimination. Fourthly, it is my religious right to keep and maintain icons of my religious beliefs. I am a convert to Argalianity, the religion of the region of Central Asia where I hunt. The Argali is the cornerstone God in our trinity. Fifthly, I am on the board of the Taxidermy Museum of America, which has a special exemption from the Endangered Species Act that allows it to gather needed specimens for its collection. They have, since my ten million donation, renamed their trophy room in my honor. Sixth, I am one of America's richest men and a leading advocate of conservation. I only took that animal with permission of the Fish and Wildlife Service to help the species survive. Seventh, I also exercised my right to barbecue it as a sacrificial offering in the tradition of the Texas branch of the Argalianity religion. And the president, himself, complimented the chef on how much Argali tastes like lamb chops.

MR. GREENWAY
I strenuously object to this unconventional list of lamb, I mean lame excuses to break the law. Are we at a trial for a man's life or a born again version of a red meat eating revival?

JUDGE
Sustained! This testimony is making me awfully hungry I know that MR.COCK.

JOHNNY
When MR. GREENWAY has his chance to cross, I assure you the answers will be even more appetizing.

JUDGE SIMBA
What could be better?

JOHNNY
Ideas pondered in the school of privilege your honor.

JUDGE SIMBA
Are you sure it wasn't pondered in a padded cell MR.COCK? It's not too late to plead insanity. Both of you that is! (Laughs all around) I apologize for my joke at your expense MR.COCK. Proceed with your case MR. COCK.

JOHNNY
Please continue MR.MOST.

EDGER
Now for my protections under the constitution and the bill of rights and various enacted laws which have been watered down to the point of being spineless devices to screw anyone with a net worth of less than ten million.

MR. GREENWAY
Object. MR.MOST is not an expert witness.

JUDGE
Sustained! We can't allow testimony that would require expert witnesses to slander freedom. MR. MOST. Any further questions.

MR COCK
No your honor.

JUDGE
Court adjourns until 9AM tomorrow.

CURTAIN DOWN/CURTAIN UP

MR.GREENWAY now cross-examines EDGER MOST. He has a haggard frustrated cheerfulness about him at the start. Before he is finished, he has the demeanor of a ruthless vengeful predatory killer.

JUDGE SIMBA

Are you ready to cross-examine the defendant Mr. Greenway?

MR. GREENWAY

I am your honor. MR.MOST, perhaps you'll begin by explaining to this court how it has come about that you consider yourself to be a member of the Negro racial group.

EDGER MOST

It would be my pleasure sir. I am of the racial stock of black Irish on three sides. I believe three-quarters black is enough to qualify one as black.

MR. GREENWAY

More than enough! And what is the forth side.

EDGER

German!

MR. GREENWAY

Was your father a hero of the Waffen SS by any chance?

EDGER

He was on General Eisenhower's staff.

MR. GREENWAY

Very interesting! We can check that. I doubt it's true. I think the SS had a General by the name of Eisenhower too though. Von Eisenhower. Are you sure it wasn't Von Eisenhower?

MR. COCK

I object to this character assassination by association your honor.

JUDGE SIMBA

Overruled!

MR. GREENWAY
Does the epithet Black Irish necessarily mean one is of the Negroid race Mr. Most?

EDGER
I can see you never served in the American military MR.GREENWAY. The choice of race is up to you in the military. At least if you're Puerto Rican.

MR. GREENWAY
(Sputtering embarrassed)
Answer the questions yes or no MR. MOST.

JUDGE SIMBA
You must answer questions yes or no MR. MOST. Please rephrase your question MR. GREENWAY

MR. GREENWAY
Are you Puerto Rican Mr. Most?

EDGER
Going by the casino table where I was conceived yes.

MR. GREENWAY
Then you claim to be black by way of being Puerto Rican rather than Black Irish?

EDGER
No.

MR. GREENWAY
Please explain Mr. Most.

EDGER
Yes.

MR.GREENWAY
You didn't explain Mr. Most.

EDGER
No.

MR. GREENWAY
Can't you answer anything but yes or no?

EDGER
Not unless God orders me to tell a lie.

MR. GREENWAY
How is that Mr. Most?

EDGER
The judge said to answer yes or no unless I can explain, although I take my orders from God. The judge does too I think.

JUDGE SIMBA
That is not true Mr. Most. In this court I am God. Answer however you feel comfortable as long as it is yes, no or you are told to explain.

EDGER
Yes your honor. As you have overruled God, as requested by MR. GREENWAY, God help him, I will try to explain. It is the black Irish that makes me black, not some military technicality. That's a racial slur. To explain, however, I will have to give you a critique of the Moorish conquest of Spain and 800 years of Moorish rule, the subsequent expulsion of the Muslim Moors by Catholic Christians, their attempted invasion of England to win it back to Catholic subjugation, the foundering on the shores of Ireland of their great invasion armada caused by a ferocious wind of the same type that saved Japan from a Chinese invasion and known today as a Kamikaze, a history of romance in Ireland since the marooning of the Armada on its shores, the potato famine resulting from the concomitant enormous increase of population and finally, a history of the migration to America of this starving nation, a genealogy search of my family to show that we are three-quarters black Irish and last but not least a DNA test to show that

my black Irish cloned ancestors originally came from Africa and were pigmies. That's why the Irish tends to be a short race. If only we had Watusi genes like the English, the Irish would have ruled the waves instead. As I am rather tall, there may have been a Watusi in the woodpile somewhere.

      MR. GREENWAY
All right MR, MOST, we concede that you are, technically speaking, black until we check your doubtful claim to be Puerto Rican. Now, why does an ARGALI sheep have to be part of your food chain? Don't Puerto Rican Negroes shop at supermarkets?

      EDGER
Shoplift more than shop.

      JUDGE SIMBA
I am Puerto Rican and I do not shoplift.

      EDGER
You better check his story too Mr. Greenway. What is your race Judge?

      JUDGE SIMBA
I am a white Puerto Rican. Pure line! Straight from the first colonists. My ancestor was first mate on the Pinto.

      EDGER
Double-check him for hoof and mouth disease in that case MR. GREENWAY.

      MR. GREENWAY
All right I will concede that only black Puerto Ricans shoplift at supermarkets.

      EDGER
You're a damn fool MR. GREENWAY.

MR. GREENWAY
I object your honor, this is contempt of court.

EDGER
It's personal contempt MR GREENWAY.

JUDGE SIMBA
Order, order in the court. You will control yourself MR. MOST. One more outburst like that and it'll be your ass sitting in jail MR. MOST.

EDGER
Can't wait to get my ass in a jail cell can you JUDGE ? Now I know why they call you JUDGE DREAD.

JUDGE SIMBA
You're in contempt of court MR. MOST. You better start stocking up on condoms. Court is in recess for one hour. MR. COCK, come to my chambers.

EDGER
If you go back there for my sake Johnny, I'll double your fee.

JUDGE SIMBA
(Knowing nod)
You can join us too Mr. Greenwood.

EDGER
Is this a trial or a short arm inspection Judge?

JUDGE
Gag this psycho until I get back.

LIGHTS DOWN/SPOT UP ON JUDGE'S CHAMBER AREA

The JUDGE and the two attorneys are meeting to decide what to do with EDGER.

JUDGE SIMBA
MR. COCK. It seems your client is not playing with a full deck. He's going to jail or the nut house if you can't control him. That's if I don't strangle him first.

MR. COCK
I'll try your honor, but he thinks paying somebody a million a day entitles him to say whatever he wants.

MR. GREENWOOD
The jury is in stitches. At the defendants expense of course.

JUDGE SIMBA
Is that assessment what you call genius MR. GREENHACK? I'm calling a recess for today! I have to think about this.

LIGHTS DOWN/SPOT UP ON COURTHOUSE STEPS AREA

JOHNNY COCK is holding an impromptu press conference on the steps of the courthouse. It is a fast pace tit for tat on the philosophical limitations of sanity. Whereas the reporters clearly think EDGER is crazy, JOHNNY expounds on an unconventional view of sanity that defines society as crazy and EDGER as crazy like a fox.

REPORTER
Is Edger Most insane?

JOHNNY
No, my client is not insane. He in fact is the sanest person I've ever met. This trial makes him appear insane, because most people misinterpret true sanity as insanity due to their own feeble grasp of reality.

REPORTER
Are you saying that most people are nuts?

JOHNNY
Most people are feeble believers in fables that keep them from being everything they can be.

REPORTER
Everyone attaches themselves to something bigger than themselves like god, a political party or a hero, but that doesn't make them insane.

JOHNNY
It makes them easy targets for manipulators.

REPORTER
You sound like a nut yourself.

JOHNNY
I'm a lawyer. I'm trained not to be a believer. We believe in nothing until we have to. That's why we run the world.

REPORTER
You think Jerry Falwell believes what he preaches?

JOHNNY
Falwell is one of the head hypocrites for my money, preaching fantasy to the suckers to protect his market share. It's all about money fellows. I gotta go guys.

REPORTER
Is Argalianity a sane religion?

JOHNNY
There is no such thing as a sane religion.

REPORTER
Then how can your client be sane?

JOHNNY
He is pseudo sane like Jerry Falwell and the rest of the moguls who manipulate the masses by taking advantage of their fear of God.

REPORTER
What is pseudo sanity?

JOHNNY
It's virtual sanity.

REPORTER
And what is real sanity.

JOHNNY
Being able to successfully live by your own rules.

REPORTER
Is that possible?

JOHNNY
It's a necessity if you want to be free. Just make sure they are the real rules.

REPORTER
Or you'll be headed for trouble.

JOHNNY
It's a guarantee of trouble.

CURTAIN DOWN/CURTAIN UP

The courtroom same as previous day. JUDGE SIMBA cites EDGER with contempt.

JUDGE SIMBA
Would the defendant please stand? Your behavior MR. MOST, most contemptuous of this court cannot go unpunished. I am taking the unusual step of sending you back to jail even though the trial is still going on. The trial will be recessed three days while you MR. MOST will have the most unusual

opportunity of meditating on what the future holds in store for you if you don't conduct yourself in a manner befitting a man on trial for his life. Take him away and try to keep him safe from those Cialis swilling aids bag prisoners you have there. The jury is instructed to in no way be prejudiced toward the defendant or judge his guilt or innocence based on this punishment. A contemptuously contemptible arrogant billionaire doth not necessarily a murderer make. The jury is recessed for three days and ordered to return at the usual time four days from now. For the record, let it be stated that this is not vengeful cruel and unusual punishment anymore as most jails today are run like x rated motels. Court adjourned until four days from today.

CURTAIN DOWN/CURTAIN UP

EDGER is in a cell by himself asleep on a bench. He wakes and speaks to the audience. At the end of the scene a Boy Scouts Scoutmaster is put in his cell much to EDGER'S chagrin

EDGER
Back again. Even after getting soaked a billion for bail. I still have quite a few billion left though, like that MILKEN crook. I think they jumped on him because he was a Jew and I because I'm a quarter German. That's what they call democracy. They sure put a high bail on killing that ARGALI lamb chop and I'm not even a serial killer... yet. It's all politics. They're only standing up for the rag heads around the world because they want access to all that oil in Central Asia. The strain of this is beginning to tell on me though. I'm having some horrible dreams again. That whole cross exam and contempt citation was a theater of the absurd surrealistic nightmare. I bet you think I am that crazy or stupid. Well, it was just a delaying tactic until I figure out my grand strategy. You bet I'll do

some thinking JUDGE DREAD. Day after tomorrow though is the real cross exam. I got to be ready. And I better watch my natural contempt for people worth less than ten million or something just as bad may happen. I can't forget that I am on trial for my life. This isn't Rashamon folks. This will be the real cross next time, so listen carefully how the rich can spin the pants off of COURTS. I'm really innocent too. No joke. Just pay close attention and you'll side with me I'm sure. You have to concentrate though if you want to connect with the big computer in the sky. You think I'm full of gray goo? We'll see. What's this? Looks like an unwelcome roommate. (Guards escort a man dressed as a Boy Scout Scoutmaster into the cell. EDGER is not too happy about this new development)

GUARD
This is SCOUTMASTER BATER your roommate for the next couple of days. (Guards exit as Edger stares at the scoutmaster in embarrassed disbelief)

EDGER
(Embarrassed)
Pleased to meet you MR. BATER. I'm EDGER.

SCOUTMASTER
My pleasure, I'm sure. What are you in for?

EDGER
Molesting, I mean killing a wild sheep.

SCOUTMASTER
(Offering hand)
Put it there partner! I'm in on a similar charge.

EDGER
Maybe I better explain.

SCOUTMASTER
No need. I'm sure you thought it was eighteen. Now, what sort of plans do you have for the weekend?

EDGER
I thought I would do a lot of thinking about what I am going to say at the trial next week.

SCOUTMASTER
Don't worry about it. Just say the kid had a false ID. That's got me off a couple dozen times.

EDGER
I think you got the wrong idea.

SCOUNTMASTER
That's a good start. Now…

CURTAIN DOWN/CURTAIN UP

Court is in session again the same as before the four-day contempt recess. The JUDGE gives EDGER a new warning and instructions before launching GREENWAY who is like a big cat that is savoring a likely kill.

CLERK
Everyone rise, the court is in session, the HONORABLE H. DREAD SIMBA presiding.

JUDGE SIMBA
Are you ready to cross-examine the defendant MR. GREENWAY?

MR. GREENWAY
The state is ready your honor.

JUDGE SIMBA
Now then MR. MOST. We hope you have learned a lesson about contempt of court. The next one will

be a lot more painful. Please answer the questions yes or no as much as possible MR. MOST and only give explanations when requested by MR. GREENWAY or myself. Understood?

EDGER
Yes SIMBA, I mean your honor.

JUDGE SIMBA
(He makes a leonine gesture yawning mouth wide and baring teeth like fangs and throwing head in a big lion like shrug)
You may precede MR. GREENWAY.

MR. GREENWAY
Now then Mr. Most, you have more or less expressed a blanket indictment of American laws by making the outrageous statement that they are watered down to being worthless. Yes or no.

EDGER
Yes in spades.

JUDGE
Careful MR.MOST!

MR. GREENWAY
Let's start with the Endangered Species Act. You are on trial for your life. What's watered down about that?

EDGER
I am charged with murder, Godicide, Sec. I, part III, paragraph IX, under some obscure 600-year-old English witchcraft law appended to the E.S.A. When they want to get you they always got some obscure law stuffed away somewhere. Look at Al Capone. Committed more murder and mayhem than anybody and they got him for income tax evasion. The accusation that I violated The Endangered Species Act has nothing to do with

this witchcraft trial. That Act was designed so that rich men like me can ignore it.

MR. GREENWAY
So you ignored this law?

MR. COCK
I object. The Act is not on trial here.

JUDGE
Overruled! Answer the question Mr. Most.

EDGER
Yes.

MR. GREENWAY
You believe, Mr. Most that you have the right to ignore laws?

MR. MOST
I change them first.

MR GREENWAY
What gives you this right Mr. Most? Explain.

EDGER
I change them based on the ponderability of privilege principle previously coined by MR.COCK. My superior resources, due to my great wealth, gain me an advantageous overview of these laws. And what is crystal clear to me is that my own rules of behavior are better than the dumb ideas cobbled together by harassed interns who are usually too busy with intimate relations to clear mindedly operate a shredder without shredding their own bras. These laws are all compromises of principle masquerading as great acts of political courage when in fact they are acts of political cowardice designed to allow the fleecing of America by large campaign contributors. In a word, these laws are worthless pacts of bribery designed to fool the gullible American public into

thinking they live in a democracy instead of a pseudocracy. The word compromise is just a euphemism for water down.

MR. GREENWAY
Do you run red lights too MR.MOST?

EDGER
Not intentionally.

MR. GREENWAY
Why not Mr. Most?

EDGER
Because it's suicide!

MR. GREENWAY
Then this prohibition is a good law?

EDGER
Sometimes!

MR. GREENWAY
When is it not?

EDGER
When cameras enforce it!

MR. GREENWAY
Why is this bad?

EDGER
Under the constitution, you are supposed to have a right to confront your accuser. Ever try confronting a camera? You have no way of defending yourself because you don't even remember the circumstances. It's just another excuse to fleece the public.

MR. GREENWAY
So you think you have a right to ignore the laws not only because they are watered down to pseudo democratic posturing, but also because they are

unconstitutional. Is that a fair characterization of your stance?

MR. COCK
I object. This is flagrant leading.

JUDGE
Overruled! You may answer MR. Most.

EDGER
Yes and no. They aren't quite the same

MR. GREENWAY
Yes and no? Please do explain.

EDGER
It is a horns of the bull attack on American democracy designed to keep the public in line to be fleeced. One horn is compromised watered down laws easy to get around and the other is garden-variety unconstitutional law too expensive to challenge. Creeping tyranny is the main thrust up the middle.

MR. GREENWAY
And you believe your superior understanding of the law gives you the right to challenge the validity of these laws by changing them to what suits you at the time. Like murder God one day and worship him the next?

MR. COCK
I object. My client is not an expert witness on the law, constitutional or otherwise.

JUDGE
Overruled, but I do think the point is being belabored by MR. GREENWAY. MR. MOST has convinced us most elegantly himself that he has no regard for any law except his own. And I say that with total impartiality. Can we go on to another line of questioning Mr. Prosecutor?

MR. GREENWAY
Thank you your honor. Now then MR.MOST, you said you are a convert to Argalianity? Was that before or after you were indicted for murder and set up a front to start this pseudo religion?

EDGER
It was by the strangest coincidence only the day before.

MR. GREENWAY
Are you sure it was a coincidence?

MR. COCK
I object to this fishing expedition. Can't the prosecutor dig up his own evidence?

JUDGE
Overruled! Answer Mr. Most.

EDGER
No

JUDGE
What do you mean no. You must answer.

EDGER
I meant no; it was not a coincidence.

JUDGE
My mistake MR.MOST! You have my profoundest apologies. Now explain before I find you in contempt.

EDGER
I wanted to celebrate my indictment for murder by bringing a new religion into the world of which I will be the founder and first martyr if I am found guilty.

JUDGE
But surely you're joking. A religion started by a murderer. The two ideas are contradictory.

EDGER
You haven't studied the history of religion have you JUDGE?

JUDGE
No. I can't say that I have MR.MOST. Please enlighten me.

EDGER
The Muslims made war and forced conversion on penalty of death their policy for expansion from the beginning, the Jews were commanded to kill all non-Jews upon entering the Promised Land and the Crusaders did the same to the Jews and Muslims that crossed their path. All religions believe they have the right to eliminate their rivals by any means including murder. That is why they should be banned.

JUDGE
But you want to start one!

EDGER
If you are one of a godhood trinity, what else can you do?

JUDGE
You may continue MR. GREENWAY.

MR. GREENWAY
Yes JUDGE. MR. MOST, first you pulled the race card and now you pull the religion card MR. MOST. Have you got any more cards in your deck we should know about MR. MOST?

EDGER
Yes. The sick card! I think I may have gotten a bad case of Bubonic Plague from the fleas in this courtroom.

The court goes into an uproar. The Judge calls for order and gets it after most of the courtroom has emptied.

JUDGE
Order, order in the courtroom. That was contemptible Mr. Most. Why didn't you cry fire and make my sanction of you simple. I will martyr you with my own hands in a minute if there are no fleas. (He starts to scratch, as do others) Guards, guards! Where are the guards? O.K! The guards are in contempt. Mr. Prosecutor. Are you still here? If you aren't, you are in contempt too. (MR. GREENWAY is crawling on the floor looking for fleas.)

MR. GREENWAY
Certainly your honor! Your honor! There are fleas.

JUDGE
I want MR. MOST taken to the hospital and given a checkup.

MR. GREENWAY
That is a job for the paramedics your honor.

JUDGE
I know you privatized stupida. The clerks and other government employees have fled. Call the paramedics and the exterminators. Don't get them mixed up or you will be in contempt. I have a flea myself. (Curses in Spanish) Court is recessed until tomorrow.

Through all this, JOHNNY sits calmly at his place. We just know where the fleas came from.

CURTAIN DOWN/CURTAIN UP

EDGER is out on bail again. JOHNNY and EDGER are meeting and laughing about the court fiasco with the fleas. JOHNNY has once again shown his genius. Or so it seems.

JOHNNY
I think court is going to have to be held standing up for a while. I don't know about the Bubonic Plague, but those butt shots are lethal.

EDGER
You were certainly calm through all this.

JOHNNY
Yeah, I've been bitten by fleas before.

EDGER
The Judge probably thinks you instigated the whole thing.

JOHNNY
Yeah, my ass is grass first time I cross him.

EDGER
How am I doing on the stand? Sorry you put me on?

JOHNNY
No, you're doing fine. They're going to hang you no matter what you say anyway. Might as well have some fun!

EDGER
That's an optimistic appraisal.

JOHNNY
I told you that you were wasting your money to hire me. I don't like to take cases I know I can't win. You're more than welcome to keep my fee and hire somebody else.

EDGER
Now don't get long winning streak battle fatigue. We are going to win and you're going to be rich.

JOHNNY
I'm already rich.

EDGER
Not really. You're only worth four or five mil. You'll be worth ten times that by the end of this trial.

JOHNNY
Yeah, yeah! I only get a million if you lose and you haven't got a prayer.

EDGER
I have one more card to play.

JOHNNY
You do! I didn't know there were anymore in a deck.

EDGER
Just be ready with your objections. This one is going to create a real row. Object to everything.

JOHNNY
Objections are a waste of breath. Judges only sustain objections against the prosecution when TV cameras are rolling and they want to pretend justice is fair and impartial.

EDGER
It slows them down a bit anyway.

JOHNNY
O.K I'm game. What's the card?

EDGER
You'll see tomorrow at Showtime.

                    JOHNNY
You know a million a day is a lot to pay a secretary.

                    EDGER
Chump change to me Johnny.

CURTAIN DOWN/CURTAIN UP

The courtroom is in session with the same cast of characters as in the last courtroom session. GREENWAY crosses MR. MOST after the judge commends Edger for saving their lives. This has GREENWAY livid with anger.

                    JUDGE
So you weren't really sick MR. MOST. But your instincts were not far off the mark. Somebody tried a bioterrorism attack on this courtroom and I am in favor of lynching, if we can find out who the culprit is. It could have been fatal too. The jail guards cited for contempt turned out to have aids and some of the homo fleas may have been infected. You have our undying gratitude for bringing those fleas to our attention MR.MOST. MR. GREENWAY, are you ready to continue the cross of this great black Puerto Rican hero?

                    MR. GREENWAY
Yes your honor. Now, you say this ARGALI sheep that you murdered and had mounted and placed as a trophy in your trophy room has now been converted into a religious icon to decorate your chapel?

                    MR. COCK
I object to the characterizations of murder and decorate.

JUDGE
Sustained with regard to murder!

MR. GREENWAY
But that is the main thing he is charged with.

JUDGE
I'm reducing the charge to manslaughter.

MR. GREENWAY
This is an animal.

JUDGE
All right! Animal slaughter.

MR. GREENWAY
That is not illegal your honor.

JUDGE
It is in my courtroom. All right, sustained as far as decorate. Continue the cross MR. GREENWAY, but keep a civil tongue in your mouth. This man is a martyr or soon will be. Too bad we don't still have crucifixion. A hero like EDGER deserves at the very least to be executed in a way that will justify a first class icon.

MR. GREENWAY
A worthy punishment I agree your honor, but it's not an option. Maybe, we can get one of our representatives in congress to slip it into a bill as an earmark. It would be just right in the new Homeland Security Bill. Nobody will ever read it anyway.

JUDGE
I like that idea Mr. Greenway. It has a certain decent panache.

MR. COCK
I object to this cockamamie bloody dialogue. My client is presumed innocent unless this court finds him guilty.

JUDGE

Sustained! We'll have to discuss this in chambers Mr. Greenway.

MR GREENWAY

Of course your honor! You say Mr. Most that you paid a twenty million dollar bribe to the American Museum of Taxidermy and they renamed it the Edger Most Museum?

MR. COCK

I object to bribe.

JUDGE

Sustained! Strike the word bribe. Answer MR. MOST.

EDGER

No sir. I donated money to the Museum and they renamed their trophy room in my honor. It's really only a temporary honor because they rename it every time there is a big donation.

MR. GREENWAY

And what sort of privileges does this entitle you too?

EDGER

Oh the usual. The right to overpay for food and drink, use of the Extinct Animal Cutout shooting range, participation in various power ball type contests for members only, playing cards for high stakes with the curator and the privilege to use the museum's exemption from a number of laws regarding the hunting and killing of rare animals.

MR. GREENWAY

One of which laws is the Endangered Species Act?

EDGER

Yes sir.

MR. GREENWAY
Are all members allowed to use these exemptions?

EDGER
No. Only worthy members.

MR. GREENWAY
Why only worthy members?

EDGER
It is up to the curator to decide who is worthy of the honor of using the museum's limited valuable exemptions.

MR. GREENWAY
Yet, you a new member were given the privilege of killing a rare ARGALI sheep. Why?

EDGER
Probably because I was a big loser at poker!

MR. GREENWAY
Which entitled you to kill this rare animal?

EDGER
Not so rare.

MR. GREENWAY
Not so rare?

EDGER
No. There were six rams left standing after I shot mine.

MR. GREENWAY
And how many females?

EDGER
Strangely, there weren't any. Maybe it was a convention of gay rams. (The court and judge find this quite amusing)

MR. GREENWAY
I find your sense of humor disgusting MR. MOST.

MR. COCK
Object! Prosecutor has no sense of humor.

JUDGE
Sustained!

MR. GREENWAY
You pray to the ARGALI?

EDGER
Yes.

MR. GREENWAY
And have your prayers been answered?

EDGER
One

MR. GREENWAY
And what is the ARGALI God granting you if you don't mind my asking

MR. COCK
Object. Self-incrimination!

JUDGE
Sustained! Rephrase the question.

MR. GREENWAY
Answer if you feel like it MR.MOST.

EDGER
He's granted me a new card to play.

MR. GREENWAY
There are only 52 in a deck. I didn't think there were any left. Is it the wild card?

MR. COCK
Object to leading…

JUDGE
Sustained, however, if you as a part of your defense strategy wish to make another defense based on answered prayers, we have no objection. How about you MR.COCK?

MR. COCK
I'm just the secretary.

JUDGE
Very strange legal maneuvering MR.COCK, even for you!

MR. COCK
And very strange judging your honor! I've never had so many objections sustained.

JUDGE
And I've never had so many made by the defense. Maybe we'll start a new fad. MR.GREENWAY, please continue.

MR. GREENWAY
What is your new god given defense card MR.MOST?

EDGER
I'm not the real EDGER MOST.

Pandemonium breaks out in the court.

JUDGE
(After bringing the court to order) Then who are you?

EDGER
I'm an exact clone copy of EDGER MOST. EDGER MOST'S number one son.

JUDGE
Where is the real EDGER MOST?

EDGER
He was a human sacrifice.

JUDGE
For what purpose?

EDGER
To stop global warming.

JUDGE
Then who shot the sheep?

EDGER
My clone cousin EDNA has confessed her culpability.

JUDGE
Why are you coming forth at this time?

EDGER
Because my cousin does not wish to make me the scapegoat for her own accidental killing of this animal, which she regrets.

JUDGE
MR. COCK, if this is another of your famous legal tricks, be prepared for the worst.

MR COCK
If it is your honor, I'll give myself a healthy raise.

JUDGE
Court is in recess until we get to the bottom of this farce. Attorneys in my chambers now!

CURTAIN DOWN/CURTAIN UP

A chapel on the MOST estate. A religious service in progress at the MOST'S chapel. The several worshippers are celebrating the ARGALI trophy mounted on the alter.

EDGER'S clone cousin, EDNA is leading this response worship service. The worshippers respond to many assertions with "Amen".

EDNA is the cloned daughter of EDGER, SR's identical twin sister who died in a hunting accident by the hand of her daughter. This daughter has a vision problem and should never be allowed to hunt. When she gets her contact lenses mixed up, she can be lethal. She is technically the twin sister of EDGER, JR.

        EDNA MOST
Dear ARGALI God in heaven, hear these your humble supplicants who love thee and wish thee a long and trouble free eternity ruling the vast reaches of the universe. May you have seventy beautiful buxom virgin ewes to comfort thee in thy lonely job of keeping the universe running smoothly for http://UUU.Universe.com/AmericaInc/subsidiaries.html/ "Amen." These ewe princesses, great, ARGALI king of the universe, have special finishing school training so that you won't get sued for sexual harassment. "Amen." Dear God, your worshippers here on this unworthy little green pasture called earth have a few small requests to beg of you before we are all burnt to a cinder. Please give the Elders of Zion a little respect and stop global warming so that they stop lobbying congress for MOSTS to be used as human sacrifices. "Amen." I know Gods have always been amused by human sacrifice, but surely you would be better amused by priests, who usually steal your sacrifice and eat it themselves, having to become vegetarians, true suffering indeed. "Amen." Please give the Bud washed no brainers better taste buds so that they vote for presidents who give a damn about global warming. "Amen." Please keep affirmative action from being repealed so that a black Irish Puerto Rican woman can become president. "Amen." And praise be to the radical conservative Supreme Court justices who

have declared the American constitution unconstitutional. "Amen." We now have church and state as partners in teaching the young religious bigotry. "Amen!" I am immediately committing a billion dollars to Church of Argali school building. We'll soon have an army of sheepherder priests. "Amen!" I just hope they aren't bad little buggers that have a taste for innocent little lambs. "Amen!" We have to be prepared for the day when non-believers have to be eliminated. Now everyone, we will sing the Ban Eating Lamb Chops goose-stepping hymn.

CURTAIN DOWN/CURTAIN UP

Back in court, same as previous, except the bailiffs are back and his identical twin clone female cousin EDNA who is dressed as a woman now replaces EDGER. This should be a real woman who looks a lot like EDGER. They are lovers and will be married.

BAILIFF
(Very swishy)
Please stand. The court is now in session. Judge H. Dread Simba presiding.

JUDGE SIMBA
My apologies everyone! The union made us take them back. Where is MR.MOST? Has he flown the coup?

MR. COCK
My turn to apologize your honor! It seems that MR. MOST, JR., with your honor's consent, has deferred to his cousin M's MOST'S wish to take responsibility for this alleged crime with which he was charged. She has decided to dress as one of her own gender and is sitting here beside me ready to testify.

JUDGE
And a big improvement it is!

EDNA
Thank you your honor.

JUDGE
You are still under oath M's Most as I have ruled that you and your cousin are the same person.

EDNA
I understand your honor.

MR. GREENWAY
The state objects to this resort to cheap tricks.

JUDGE
Overruled! I have ruled that all MOST clones are interchangeable and must bear equal responsibility for the death of the ARGALI if convicted. You may proceed with the cross MR.GREENHACK unless you want to rest your case.

MR. GREENWAY
It's GREENWAY your honor. GREENWAY! All right, I will continue. I don't get paid for incompetence like most government employees. Mr., I mean M's MOST, do you think that just because you are a women you have the affirmative right to be treated any differently by the law than if you were a man?

EDNA
Most certainly MR.GREENHACK!

MR. GREENWAY
You see what you started HORNELIA D. SIMBA?

JUDGE
It's GREENWAY M'S MOST. Please.

EDNA
Sorry.

MR. GREENWAY
In what way M's MOST are you treated differently?

EDNA
For the same reason that auto mechanics treat us differently.

MR. GREENWAY
How do they treat you?

EDNA
They cheat us.

MR. GREENWAY
They cheat everybody.

EDNA
So does the law.

MR. GREENWAY
It's the same for everybody.

JUDGE
Mr. Greenway, you are out of order. The law cheats Puerto Ricans more than Anglos.

MR. GREENWAY
Not when you try to get food stamps.

JUDGE
Anglos get too much to eat anyway. Everybody knows that.

MR. GREENWAY
I object.

JUDGE
Overruled!

MR. GREENWAY
Overruled! Overruled! Is that the only word of English you know? Judges almost never overrule prosecutors. This is blatant favoritism. Who appointed you? Must have been Clinton, because you're as bad a womanizer as he was! You're almost salivating over this perverted clone.

JUDGE
You're in contempt MR. GREENWAY. Bailiffs, restrain this slanderer, this privatisimo prick. There are some things that should be owned by the public and prosecution is one of them.

MR. GREENWAY
You dare attack the great-privatized Orange, County American legal system?

JUDGE
Viva Castro. Free Puerto Rico. Give the Mexicans back the southwest.

MR.GREENWAY
They already got it you little wetback shoplifter. We did do a check.

BAILIFF
(Sitting on Greenway) What do we do with him your honor?

JUDGE
What you usually do to bad prisoners I would guess. Give them a long shower.

MR. GREENWAY
Unhand me you brutes. I am not a prisoner yet.

BAILIFF
Not yet sweetie, but you will be soon.

JUDGE
Forget the shower. Keep him in bailiff's lockup tonight. I forgot; I'm for cruel and unusual punishment. The court is recessed.

MR. GREENWAY
The prosecution rests its case.

JUDGE
There's still closing arguments. Have yours ready tomorrow MR. GREENWAY if you have time in your busy schedule tonight. You too, Mr. Cock! Court adjourned.

EDNA
Boys will be boys.

CURTAIN DOWN/CURTAIN UP

The Elders of Zion are having another meeting to decide the fate of humanity.

HELGA
I Grand Potentate MEGAWORT call The Elders of Zion to order on this 35th day of Juno in the year 5294.

MANFRIED
There are only 31 days in a month at the most give or take a couple, you dumkopf Helga Megavart.

HELGA
You count on your fingers like a bud goy little Pippick.

MANFRIED
Well, I know how to count to 5295, because Jesus told me so.

ARNOLD
It's 5293 years old too or you must be a Jew for Jesus Republican Pippickweisser.

MANFRIED
You wait till Jesus comes back Rosenvelt. You're headed for a holocaust that'll make the other one seem like a girl-scout campfire.

HELGA
You two must have had your brains fumigated at one of L.A.s' hydrochloric acid high school campuses.

MANFRIED
Vatch your devious lies Helga. Tell her Rosenvelt.

ARNOLD
Vatch whatch you say Helga. With lies you tell, no vonder ve don't get no respect.

Both men are wearing Belmont High Toxics T-shirts when they turn toward camera/audience.

HELGA
Are ve going to put a stop to global warming here or have a lynching revival?

MANFRIED
Are we going to lynch most Edger Mosts or not?

HELGA
No dummy. Only vags get lynched anymore.

MANFRIED
You mean fags.

HELGA
No, I mean vags. Skin head actors that are in that penis contortion play.

MANFRIED
Their schlongs look like pretzels. But why?

HELGA

They can show off the Swastikas tattooed on their schlongs.

ARNOLD

Who lynches them?

HELGA

The IRS.

ARNOLD

I thought they were pussies.

HELGA

Not anymore. The President has given them 007 statuses since 9/11.

MANFRIED

Would it be possible to get some work done?

HELGA

Things look bad. EDGER MOST, JR and the Judge are both Puerto Ricans.

ARNOLD

Yeah, but the Judge is white and Edger is black!

MANFRIED

That's just a military friction.

HELGA

Maybe there's still hope. How about a backup plan? EDNA is a clone. Let's orchestrate a lynching of the real EDGER MOST posthumously for cloning himself as a woman. And she probably abuses herself too. It's a lynching offense.

MANFRIED

But she is the daughter of his identical twin sister who was killed by EDNA in a hunting accident.

HELGA

That's another military friction. I'm for burning at the stake.

ARNOLD
No, that is too goy. Let's get a restraining order on MOSTS cloning another embryo. Then they won't have eternal life any more.

ALL THREE
(They all three dance around like witches again) That's it. That's it. Edger Most is toast. Edger Most is toast. And so is Edna Most. (Repeat)

CURTAIN DOWN/CURTAIN UP

Dude Sixpac and Mary Bimbat are in bed eating popcorn and watching the election returns on TV. No sports are on as all the stations have preempted sports programming to follow the returns.

DUDE
Make sure that popcorn goes in your mouth honey. Every time we eat it in bed I end up with popcorn in the crack of my ass for a week.

MARY
Don't worry Dude honey. It's my turn to be on the bottom.

DUDE
Yeah and you get it in the same place.

MARY
Try peeing through popcorn if you think you got it hard.

DUDE
Can you believe they preempted all the games for this election crap?

MARY
They do it every election. Want another Bud?

DUDE
Does the Pope look like he needs stem cells?

MARY
Who's winning?

DUDE
Winning what? They preempted everything.

MARY
The election Dude!

DUDE
Who cares?

MARY
I thought you voted for the one that drank Bud.

DUDE
I did.

MARY
Don't you care whether he wins?

DUDE
Nah! They're all bozos, even if they drink Rollin Rock. Speaking of Rollin, that gives me an idea. Roll over. I want to try peeing through the popcorn with you.

MARY
Dude baby... Let's chug-a-lug a few more Buds first!

DUDE
Aren't you worried about a gusher?

MARY
That's better than a dry whole.

DUDE
It's your call.

                        MARY
            Let's flip.

                        DUDE
            O.K. heads or tails?

                        MARY
            I'll take tails.

                        DUDE
            You win again.

                        MARY
            Again! This coin is fixed. O.K., roll over. I'll strap
            on the autographed football.

She pulls out a large dildo with a football shaped head and autographed by Joe Nameth. .

CURTAIN DOWN/CURTAIN UP

Court is in session same as previous courtroom session. JUDGE SIMBA exonerates the prosecutor and agrees to a new prosecution witness. The prosecution is pulling out all the stops and has plans to win by hook or crook. Mostly crook.

                        JUDGE SIMBA
            Are you ready to make your closing argument MR,
            GREENWAY?

                        MR. GREENWAY
            I am your honor.

                        JUDGE SIMBA
            I trust you got plenty of rest?

                        MR. GREENWAY
            None your honor!

JUDGE
Did the bailiffs keep you up all night reading you bedtime stories?

MR GREENWAY
Your honor, I object to your insinuation. I spent the whole night working on my closing speech. The bailiffs were in the other bunk.

JUDGE
I release you from my sanction MR.GREENWAY and admonish the guards that it is a good thing there wasn't any hanky-panky. This just proves the bad rap our jails get is all just a lot of hype to elicit sympathy for criminals. I commend you MR.GREENWAY for going undercover and proving that the media liberals are all liars. I apologize if my Puerto Rican temper got the best of me and I inadvertently exposed you to any danger. I thought it would be a feather in your bonnet to see how the justice system works from the inside.

MR. GREENWAY
It was more fun than a trip to Tijuana your honor. The court will get a small bill for overtime at 500 an hour. I trust that's O.K. with you your honor.

JUDGE
It's all part of privatization economics MR.GREENWAY. I have to support the system I uphold don't I? Now can we proceed with the closing argument MR.GREENWAY?

MR. GREENWAY
The state has another witness your honor.

JUDGE
This better be important MR. GREENWAY. The dock is overflowing with other prisoners who would like to have their day in court.

JOHNNY
I strenuously object to this Perry Mason grandstanding, your honor.

JUDGE
So do I, but we must indulge prosecutors now and again. MR.GREENWAY, speak to me in my chambers. MR. COCK, join us.

LIGHTS DOWN/ SPOT ON JUDGE'S CHAMBER AREA

MR. GREENWAY and MR.COCK join the JUDGE in his chambers.

JUDGE
Now, MR.GREENWAY! Why do you want to persecute this holy Puerto Rican hero with a new witness?

MR. GREENWAY
Because I am being paid by the people to win this case, believe it or not your honor.

JUDGE
Fair enough! Who is this witness?

MR. GREENWAY
MR. JERIMIAH BATER.

JUDGE
Oh yes SCOUTMASTER BATER. I've seen him on the dock. And how many pieces of silver have you promised MR. BATER to be the state's witness, MR. GREENWAY?

JOHNNY
Who is this Mr. Scout MasterBater? Did I get that right?

JUDGE

If I said yes, I'd have to recuse myself from this case and I want it bad. MR. BATER was your client's cellmate when I cited him for contempt.

JOHNNY

This is a travesty. The judge asked you what you promised to give him, GREENWAY.

MR. GREENWAY

We have determined that SCOUTMASTER BATER was ganged raped by his scout troop. Therefore the charges against him will probably be dropped.

JOHNNY

I don't believe this!

JUDGE

I will handle this MR. COCK. What evidence does MR. BATER have to offer that could be important enough for the bench to reopen your well-rested case, MR. GREENWAY?

MR. GREENWAY

MR. MOST confessed to MR. BATER, not only all the charges against him, but of being a terrorist confederate of Osama bin Laden. Do you really believe that MR. MOST was in Central Asia just to hunt sheep? He's an arms smuggler for the terrorists. How do you think he became so rich?

JUDGE

O.K.! You got me on this one. Is your witness ready?

MR. GREENWAY

He will be in the morning.

JOHNNY

I protest your honor.

JUDGE
Sorry MR. COCK. We've got to find out the truth about this. The press will crucify me if this is true and I don't allow this witness. I'm sure you can get to the bottom of this accusation MR. COCK. I'm adjourning till tomorrow. Be ready. Both of you! And this better not be a hoax MR. GREENWAY

CURTAIN DOWN/CURTAIN UP

The courtroom is the same as the previous scene except for a new witness. The new witness, SCOUTMASTER BATER is put on the stand the next morning. MR. GREENWAY is questioning him followed by MR. COCK.

MR. GREENWAY
MR. BATER, you are a man, who teaches others to tell the truth, are you not?

MR. BATER
As a scoutmaster, truth is a big part of the creed we teach the kids, yes.

MR. GREENWAY
"On a scout's honor", is the essence of that creed isn't it?

MR. BATER
Yes sir.

MR. GREENWAY
Now, I know the court knows you know you are under oath here to tell the truth, but just to emphasize this fact, do you also swear on a scouts honor that your testimony will be true?

MR. BATER
Yes sir, I swear on a scouts honor.

MR. GREENWAY
Do you see MR. EDGER MOST in this courtroom?

MR. BATER
Yes sir.

MR. GREENWAY
How do you know MR MOST?

MR. BATER
We shared a cell together for three days recently.

MR. GREENWAY.
I see. Are you now free?

MR. BATER
Yes sir.

MR. GREENWAY
Why are you free?

MR. BATER
All charges against me have been dropped.

MR. GREENWAY
And why were they dropped.

MR. BATER
My accusers admitted, when confronted with medical evidence, that they were the molesters and I was the molested.

MR. COCK
I object to this hearsay.

MR. GREENWAY
I offer this medical report in evidence your honor.

JUDGE
(Looks at report)
This seems to be official. You are overruled MR. COCK. Please continue MR.GREENWAY.

MR. GREENWAY
Did the state make you any promises in return for your testimony here today, MR.BATER?

MR. BATER
No sir.

MR. GREENWAY
When you and MR.MOST were cellmates, were you on friendly terms?

MR. BATER
Yes.

MR. GREENWAY
Intimate terms?

MR. BATER
Yes.

MR. GREENWAY
In moments of passion, did Mr. or should I say M'S MOST open up to you and share his-her deepest secrets?

MR. COCK
I object. M'S MOST had not yet entered this case.

JUDGE
What is this innuendo MR. GREENWAY?

MR. GREENWAY
As the defendant is an exact copy except for gender, it could have been most any MOST. For all we know, there may be more MOSTS.

JUDGE
Overruled MR.COCK. Your client's gender is not important. You may answer Scoutmaster.

MR. BATER
Yes, she opened in more ways than one. She sang her hotti little heart out like a love-starved slut marooned solo on a desert island for ten years.

MR. GREENWAY
Did he-she tell you what he-she was doing in Central Asia?

MR. BATER
Yes.

MR. GREENWAY
Can you tell us in your own words?

MR. BATER
He said she was a C.I.A. agent who was sent to Central Asia to find Osama bin Laden and find out what he was doing. The sheep hunting was just a cover story.

MR. GREENWAY
Did he find Osama bin Laden?

MR. BATER
Yes. He met him.

MR. GREENWAY
I'm surprised he lived to tell the tail. Can you tell us how he survived this meeting?

MR. BATER
He agreed to become a double agent.

MR. GREENWAY
A mole for the terrorists?

MR. BATER
Yes.

MR. GREENWAY
He was paid for this information?

MR. BATER
Yes, billions.

MR. GREENWAY
That's how he made so much money?

MR. BATER
He also made it smuggling drugs, weapons for the terrorists on C.I.A. planes, pirating software, movies, you name it, and he had his hand in it.

MR. GREENWAY
And the Argali sheep he claims to worship?

MR. BATER
He's strictly a trophy hunter trying to get a gold ring from the Safari club.

MR. GREENWAY
The prosecution rests its case your honor.

JUDGE
Thank you MR. GREENWAY! I think from now on I'm going to claim my ancestor was first mate of the Mayflower. Your witness MR.COCK!

MR. COCK
Thank you your honor. Now, MR. BATER, you took this Boy Scout troop to a month long jamboree in the wilderness of Sequoia National Park?

MR. BATER
Yes.

MR. COCK
And you claim you were molested?

MR. BATER
Raped would be a better description.

MR. COCK
How many were in the troop?

MR. BATER
Ten at that time I think. A few had dropped out along the way. Normal attrition.

MR. COCK
And how many were involved in what you call a rape?

MR. BADER
All ten.

MR. COCK
And what was the age range?

MR. BADER
About twelve to sixteen.

MR COCK
How long were you there before the big event?

MR. BADER
About three weeks.

MR. COCK
What sort of activities went on?

MR. BADER
The usual scout activities. Camping in tents, swimming, hiking, singing around the camp fire…

MR. COCK
Everything normal… did you skinny dip when swimming?

MR. BADER
It wasn't a requirement, but it's popular with kids that age.

MR. COCK
Yes or no Mr. Bader?

MR. BADER
Yes.

MR. COCK
Is that normal?

MR. BADER
No rule prohibits it.

MR. COCK
Did you notice anything abnormal about these kids before the big event?

MR. BADER
Did you ever see the movie, "The Lord of the Flies"?

MR. COCK
Yes. Why?

MR. BADER
That loosening of civilized inhibitions is what was happening, but I didn't realize it until too late. Some of these kids had sneak watched porno on the net and were living in a sexual fantasy world. Their raging teen hormones got the best of them.

MR. COCK
And you did nothing to provoke this?

MR. BADER
Of course not!

MR. COCK
You, a grown man were unable to fight off this bunch of horny kids?

MR. BATER
They drugged my coffee with ecstasy and who knows what else. I was helpless. The medical report will give you the details.

MR. COCK
Are you sure you didn't take those drugs yourself?

MR. BATER
No. They found them in the kid's pockets.

MR. COCK
Why were you arrested, if they found the drugs in the kid's pockets?

MR. BADER
They didn't find them until after the medical report.

MR. COCK
Who obtained this report and ordered this search?

MR. BADER
My court appointed attorney.

MR. COCK
To prepare for a plea bargain?

MR. BADER
He said he was being offered a deal for my honest testimony in this case.

MR. COCK
Which has been true on your scouts honor?

MR. BATER
You bet.

MR. COCK
Are you homosexual Mr. Bader?

MR. BADER
God no!

MR. COCK
You suggested that you had sex with Edger Most in jail?

MR. BADER
Yes.

MR. COCK
But you thought MR.MOST was a man.

MR. BADER
He said he was a killer and I was frightened.

MR. COCK
You claim he fell for you and spilled his guts.

MR. BADER
That is correct.

MR. COCK
All the things you claim MR.MOST or M'S MOST told you about what he or she were doing in Central Asia are just your word against his. You have no other proof. Am I correct?

MR. BADER
You are incorrect.

MR. COCK
How so Mr. Bader?

MR. BADER
Take a good look at this picture I tore out of the current issue of Taxidermy Magazine. It has a picture of EDGER MOST and OSAMA bin LADEN by the Argali. (Holds up picture and MR. COCK takes it from him)

MR. COCK
Your honor, I request a recess. This blindsiding me with such a crucial piece of evidence is grounds for a mistrial.

JUDGE
Trial recessed until morning. Gentleman, in my chambers and bring that picture.

<u>LIGHTS DOWN/UP ON JUDGE'S CHAMBER AREA.</u>

The judge, the prosecutor and Mr. Cock are in meeting.

JUDGE
How could you pull such a crude trick on this court MR. GREENGENIUS??

MR. GREENWAY
I swear to you, I had nothing to do with this. That guys a loose canon.

MR. COCK
Nobody will believe you GREENHACK.

MR. GREENWAY
All right! What do you want?

MR. COCK
I'm going to have to put my client back on the stand to prove how he got away from bin Laden's murderers without being compromised.

MR. GREENWAY
That'll be a good trick since bin Laden kills anybody not on his side.

JUDGE
O.K. We'll hear from MR. MOST for the last time I hope.

CURTAIN DOWN/ CURTAIN UP

The trial is back in session the next morning with EDGER MOST sworn in. He is questioned by MR. COCK and crossed by MR.GREENWAY.

JUDGE
O.K., MR MOST, you are under oath and the same rules apply as during your last testimony. Your client MR. COCK.

MR. COCK
Is this a picture of you and Osama bin Laden?

EDGER MOST
Yes.

MR. COCK
How did you meet MR. BIN LADEN?

EDGER
After I shot the Argali, he appeared out of nowhere and claimed he shot at me by mistake and wanted to apologize.

MR. COCK
So the two of you were friendly when the natives showed up?

EDGER
Yes. That's why the picture taking.

MR. COCK
When did you find out who he was?

EDGER
When you told me it was he in this picture.

MR. COCK
So you could not have told MR. BADER you had known MR. Bin LADEN or worked for the terrorists.

EDGER
Correct.

MR. COCK
How did you escape from your death sentence?

EDGER
These were followers of the DELI TEK who had personally authorized my hunting the Argali for religious reasons. When he heard about my sentence he pardoned me. Of course, that cost me another ten million.

MR. COCK
Tell us what happened between you and MR. BADER in jail. Did the two of you have sex?

EDGER
No, although he tried to molest me.

MR. COCK
What form did this take?

EDGER
Blackmail. He said he would testify against me, if I did not have sex with him.

MR. COCK
That's all the questions I have your honor.

JUDGE
Well, I'm starting to feel good about looking at myself in the mirror again. I suppose you want to cross MR. GREENWOOD?

MR. GREENWOOD
You bet I do. You certainly have a lot of millions to spread around MR. MOST. Where do they come from if not from OSAMA bin LADEN?

EDGER
I was a venture capitalist investor during the dot com bubble, but I quickly took my profits and ran before the bubble burst. I made tens of billions. This whole fiasco has only cost me around a hundred million, chump change when you get over a billion a year in interest on your money like I do.

MR. GREENWOOD
What would you say if Mosad had supplied us with a cancelled check signed by bin Laden and made out to you for a billion?

EDGER
I'd say it's a forgery, since the terrorists are not known to use checks.

MR. GREENWOOD
You claim you never had sex with MR. BADER while incarcerated?

EDGER
That's right.

MR. GREENWOOD
Why not, you're a woman aren't you?

EDGER
You're confusing me with my cousin EDNA

MR. GREENWOOD
Are you sure she wasn't the one in jail who had sex with BADER ?

EDGER
She isn't a boy scout.

MR. GREENWOOD
That's all the questions I have your honor.

JUDGE
Does the defense want a re-cross?

MR. COCK
No your honor, but I have another witness.

JUDGE
Side bar gentleman!
(The lawyers at side bar)

JUDGE
What is the meaning of this MR.COCK? You got him beat by a mile.

MR. COCK
Yes, but I promised the big truth and this witness will provide it.

JUDGE
O.K. Last one for both of you. Who is it MR.COCK?

MR. COCK
One of the Boy Scouts in Scoutmaster Bader's troop has agreed to testify.

MR. GREENWAY
I object to bringing a minor into this court that may be charged with a major crime.

JUDGE
Overruled MR. GREENWAY! Is the witness ready MR. COCK?

MR. COCK
Yes he is your honor.

JUDGE
Put him on the stand MR. COCK.
(The players return to their places and MR. COCK calls his witness)

MR. COCK
The defense calls MR. ADAM BIRD.
(A young man about sixteen takes the stand and is sworn in)

MR. COCK
MR. BIRD, will you tell in your own words what happened on the morning of July 5?

MR. BIRD
The day started like every other day at camp. We had our morning skinny dip and then a hardy breakfast. After breakfast, we were given pills to take.

MR. COCK
Was this unusual?

MR. BIRD
No sir. Except they weren't just vitamin pills as usual! The scoutmaster said we were going on a long sweaty hike in rattlesnake infested areas and must take salt pills and anti snake bite pills in addition to the vitamins.

MR. COCK
Can you describe the salt pill and the Anti-snake pill?

MR. BIRD
Well, the salt pill was a little round red pill and the other was a diamond shaped blue pill.

MR. COCK
How old are you Mr. Bird?

MR. BIRD
Sixteen sir.

MR. COCK
Have you ever seen these kinds of pills before?

MR. BIRD
Yes.

MR. COCK
Where?

MR. BIRD
They were the same as the ones the police found when they searched my camp baggage.

MR. COCK
Do you know how they got there?

MR. BIRD
No sir.

MR. COCK
Who handed out the pills on the morning of the hike?

MR BIRD
The scoutmaster.

MR. COCK
Do you know Viagra when you see it?

MR. BIRD
No sir.

MR. COCK
Did you know salt pills are white and taste salty?

MR. BIRD
No sir.

MR. COCK
I have no further questions your honor.

JUDGE
Cross MR. GREENWAY?

MR. GREENWAY
Very nice story young man! Haven't you been arrested for possession of those red pills, which were ecstasy?

MR. BIRD
Yes sir.

MR. GREENWAY
Weren't bottles filled with these substances passed from hand to hand?

MR. BIRD
Yes sir.

MR. GREENWAY
So you are not sure whom you got these pills from. Bottles could have been switched couldn't they have?

MR. BIRD
Not likely Sir.

MR. GREENWAY
Why not?

MR. BIRD
We were all afraid of snakes.

MR. GREENWAY
You are one of those accused of attacking MR. BADER, are you not?

MR. BIRD
Yes sir.

MR. GREENWAY
Did MR. BADER do anything to provoke this behavior?

MR. BIRD
No sir.

MR. GREENWAY
No more questions your honor.

JUDGE
Re-cross MR. COCK.

MR. COCK
Yes. MR. BIRD, you say MR. BADER did nothing to provoke the actions of yourself and your fellow campmates.

MR. BIRD
Yes.

MR. COCK
Had he ever made any sexual advances to anyone?

MR. BIRD
He and a gay scout had a fling affair.

MR. COCK
So it was known to the troop that MR, BADER was a child molester?

MR. BIRD
We didn't look at it that way. There are gay kids you know. And MR. BADER was always nice to us. Nobody wanted to rat them out. It wasn't considered to be cool.

MR. COCK
When this alleged rape happened, what was going on?

MR. BIRD
We were all high on something and MR. BADER suggested we go skinny dipping in the pond to chill out.

MR. COCK
What did MR. BADER do?

MR. BIRD
He went skinny dipping with us.

MR. COCK
Was this unusual?

MR. BIRD
Yes.

MR. COCK
Why?

MR. BIRD
Because he and the gay kid usually went off some place.

MR. COCK
And on this occasion?

MR. BIRD
The kid had gone home because he was sick. I hear he had gonorrhea.

MR. COCK
Have you and your friends contracted gonorrhea since the alleged rape.

MR. BIRD
Some of us.

MR. COCK
Have you?

MR. BIRD
Yes sir.

MR. COCK
Thank you MR. BIRD. That's all the questions your honor.

JUDGE
Re-cross MR. GREENWAY

MR. GREENWAY
Yes. Have you dated since the alleged rape MR. BIRD?

MR. BIRD
Yes sir.

MR. GREENWAY
And was it a woman?

MR. BIRD
Yes sir. My steady girl friend.

MR. GREENWAY
Have you had sex with her?

MR. BIRD
Yes.

MR. GREENWAY
And does she have gonorrhea?

MR. BIRD
We don't know. She has gotten preventive penicillin shots since I discovered what I have.

MR. GREENWAY
So there is no way to prove whom you got the clap from is there MR, BIRD?

MR. BIRD
No sir.

MR. GREENWAY
The state rests its case again your honor.

JUDGE
Halleluiah! Have your closing arguments ready in the morning gentleman. Courts adjourned until 9AM tomorrow.

CURTAIN DOWN/CURTAIN UP

Closing arguments are heard. The prosecution goes first.

JUDGE
All right Mr. Prosecutor, are you ready to present the people's closing statement?

MR. GREENWAY
I am your honor.

JUDGE
Then proceed, MR. GREENWAY.

MR. GREENWAY
Yes your honor. Ladies and Gentlemen of the court! We have heard the defendant pull one trump card out of the deck after another to try to convince this court that he did not commit a premeditated act of murder when he bushwhacked that innocent protected ARGALI ram that was a God to the people of Inner Taztikistan. MR. MOST, who as it

turns out is now M's Most has the temerity to claim this was all an accident as his, I mean her gun discharged by mistake when he was protecting the Argali from predators other than himself. If we were to accept accident as a valid excuse for prohibited killing, no killer in the world would be found guilty. She backs up this claim by claiming to be a follower of Argalianity, the Taztikistan state religion. She premeditatedly murdered the poor beast and now pretends to be a worshipper of him to save her own hide. On top of this, there are other laws she is charged and not charged with breaking that have been not only broken, but the defendant flaunts the fact that she believes she has a divine duty to break these bad laws. Number one is the Endangered Species Act that he, I mean she, characterizes as a watered down law designed to favor millionaires. She claims that an exemption to the prohibition of hunting endangered species held by his hunting club not only entitles her to hunt this rare animal, it entitles him to break other similarly watered down laws. This flawed female logic challenges all our most sacred legislative traditions in this country. Without the device of compromise, almost no law in the history of this country would have been passed. Just because laws have more holes in them than a Hollywood movie does not make them bad laws. This colander like design keeps them from becoming soggy like over soaked pasta. Sometimes there are inadvertent flaws of course. Busy congressional interns do make mistakes even if they aren't wearing a bra. Fortunately we have a system where the president, by executive order, can correct these unintended loopholes. He did this just before M'MOST accidentally on purpose murdered the ARGALI. The fact that M'S MOST'S club was not informed as were many others is most unfortunate, but ignorance of the law is never an excuse. A copy of the backdated order auto signed by the president is exhibit 14 along with many cartons of proof that this was not done ex post facto. M'S. MOST'S slander of the American legislative system must not go unpunished, however, and we ask you to bring a verdict of murder one, as we believe this whole international incident was a setup perpetrated by M's Most to discredit America and its institutions. M's Most is suspected of being a die-hard communist. If you just stop and ruminate on the similarities, you will see that corporations, several of which are controlled by the MOST clones, are in many ways very similar in organization to communist countries. The defendant M'S MOST is not a real human being either. She is an illegal clone created from embryos procreated for the single purpose of giving Edger-Edna Most maximum eternal sexual fulfillment. This procedure is considered murder in almost every country except Taztikistan and other backward theocracies. M's MOST, not satisfied with the current endless roster of offenses she is charged with has come up with a new twist. She is the first transgender human clone. For some absurd reason known only to EDGER MOST, SR, deceased, he has upped the illegal cloning ante another notch by having himself cloned as a female. This has lead to the breeding of this despicable murderer who is sitting here before you. If this were not repugnant enough, she claims to be of the Negroid race by way of being black Irish Puerto Rican. She claims that as a black person, she has the right to, as it were, make up for lost time when blacks were denied the same privileges as whites. I ask you in all seriousness, when has the killing of a God and the perversion of democratic principles been a white only privilege? Not in any history book I have read. And last but by no means least, SCOUTMASTER BADER has not only confirmed that she is a premeditated murderer of protected animals sacred to many people, but is a terrorist confederate of OSAMA bin LADEN. I ask this court then to find the defendant guilty as charged on all counts, which are almost countless. And if she pulls the pregnancy card, I say hang all three.

JUDGE
Bully ending MR. GREENWAY. Just be careful if you get a prosecuting gig in Puerto Rico. You might have your cajones deprivatized and used for a gag. MR. COCK, I trust you are ready to come to the aid of MOST? Sorry about the bad pun MR. COCK. Are you representing MR. OR M'S MOST?

MR. COCK
All of them your honor!

JUDGE
Then proceed Mr. Cock!

MR.COCK
Honorable JUDGE SIMBA and Ladies and Gentleman of the COURT. I am tempted to rest my case right here, because I think the prosecutor has done a wonderful job of proving the innocence of my client all by himself without any help from me. But to be honest, my ego will not allow me to rest without adding to the many reasons cited by MR. GREENWAY why my client deserves to be found innocent. After all, we owe it to future generations to tell the truth, the whole truth and nothing but the truth because the truth will set us all free they say. Trouble with that is it has to be the whole truth. Almost all our troubles in this world stem from the truth being parceled out in parsimonious parcels too chintzy to do anybody any good. That's why somebody needs to tell the big truth. I am here to tell you that whole big truth. First, let's consider the matter of women and firearms. Should they be held to the same strict

standards as men? We concede this to be the case. It is estimated that as many as 5000 men a year are killed in hunting accidents involving accidental discharge of weapons and many more in cases of mistaken identity. M'S MOST claims her accidental discharge happened because she thought the coiled antlers of the Argali were in reality a coiled snake poised to attack. In Tastikistan folklore, there is a tail that asserts that those coiled horns of the Argali are the result of just such an attack. The Argali's God turned a snake to stone just as its fangs pierced the head of an ordinary ram. The god admiring the new found beauty of the ram decided to live in its body. Consequently, this divine mutation forever after has been fused to the head and soul of the divine Argali. This was therefore an accident waiting to happen. M'S MOST, as luck would have it, lost one of her contact lenses that very same morning, as she usually does. Not having a spare she naturally was seeing double and triple interweaving each other. Because of her congenital spiral vision, she was startled upon being confronted by what appeared to be a coiled snake ready to attack and consequently shot the Argali god by mistake. As far as her conversion to the Taztikistan state religion is concerned, this happened long before going to Taztikistan. As a young CIA intern, she met the head of the Argalianity religion at CIA headquarters in Washington, D.C. where her job was debriefing important political refugees in such a way as to win them over to freedom. The DELI TEK, who had gone to pick up his C.I.A. paycheck and be debriefed, was so impressed with M'S MOST he made an instant convert out of her. Of course, he didn't make it official until the day before M'S MOST'S indictment. National security considerations prevent disclosing more details about this debriefing method. Don't believe any of that rot about a culture of pseudo celibacy among Argali monks, although I'm sure there are many supermarket tabloids and Internet sites that claim to show lurid details of the full bogus story. Of course she was assumed to be a man then, albeit with female side of brain spiritual propensities toward celibate monks. In the matter of SCOUTMASTER BADER'S claims that she admitted to shooting the Argali as a cover story for being on a terrorist mission for Osama bin Laden, the truth has been revealed in a recent video released by Mr. bin Laden. He has revealed that it was he who really shot the Argali by mistake when he was trying to shoot her. M'S MOST is willing to submit to a thorough Wen Ho Lee type of F.B.I investigation to prove she is a respecter of the laws and loyal to this country in every way. All of this has been validated as true by a do it yourself polygraph test kit she has used that is available on the Internet from Polygraph.com, a subsidiary of the Church of Argali. He-she has also donated another twenty million to be divided up by members of congress for their reelection campaigns. Since it has never been proven that M'S MOST'S mother's egg was fertilized by Puerto Rican sperm, a proposed law has been put on fast track to give black Irish the option of being legally of the Negroid race if they wish. Allegations of her contempt for the compromise process by which most laws are passed in this country find that 70% of people polled feel the same way. No doubt congress out of deep respect for majority rule will in the not too distant future declare all federal laws bastardized and pass an entire new set of laws more in line with the overwhelming polled wishes of the electorate. As there is no proof that M's Most has broken any of the laws she is charged or not charged with breaking, she should be found innocent of all charges and set free to continue her conservation efforts that has saved the left footed praying mantis from certain extinction. Last but not least, she is dedicated to a life of breaking the laws that her civic instinct tells her are bad laws. It is everyone's duty to break such laws. However, to date she has not broken any law. Thank you.

CURTAIN DOWN/ CURTAIN UP

The courtroom same as previous scene. The court has returned after reaching a verdict. The judge reads his verdict. The whole Most clan is found not guilty by way of insanity even though the charge was murder. Edger and Edna happily embrace in a hot amorous kiss that gives away the fact that they are lovers. They are soon married and provoke the greatest controversy in American history.

BAILIFF
(The judge enters) The honorable JUDGE H. DREAD SIMBA presiding. The court stand.

JUDGE SIMBA
This court has reached a verdict of not guilty to the charge of murder by way of insanity of the whole MOST clan and their attorney. The defendants are released. I just hope there is a paddy wagon waiting.

CURTAIN DOWN/CURTAIN UP ON POND

A stream through a coastal wetland. This should be possible with proper flats and other props. It can be just a pond.

Edna Most is decked out in a safari suit, as was Edger Most in the first scene. She now is equipped with a net and is trying to catch something in a pond. She reveals that she and Edger have been married and holds up a gold Safari club ring that is her wedding ring from Edger.

EDNA
You know these fast snail darters are really hard to find. No wonder scientists claim they are

endangered. I am trying to collect one for our endangered species museum to complete the collection of rare species EDGER and I have captured. People are flocking to our museum in droves to see the only complete collection of rare species specimens in the world. You are invited too. Where else can you see all the rare species under one roof? Disney is building a rare animal theme park and so are a few others, but we have the first. I've endowed it with 10 billion, so it's almost free to the public. Of course it's called somewhat ironically the EDNA and EDGER MOST Rare Species Museum, a theme park subsidiary of the Church of Argali. Come on out and see me. It's special to me because EDGER and I were married there in the chapel by his holiness the DELI TEK himself. And EDGER gave me his own Safari club gold ring as a wedding ring. (Holds it up to see) And DELI doesn't need that million a year stipend from the CIA anymore either since the communists got the boot. His country is back under his yoke and he's cleaning up. Bye, bye fellow billionaires and you other folk hang in there. Your turn will come.

FINI

REVEREND MONEY

A Comedy

Written

BY

ED WODE

Copyright © 2006
by Ed Wode
*** See disclaimer note at end of play
edwode@gmail.com

REVEREND MONEY

A man made up in the mode of a Kabuki actor with a Kabuki hair wig and face painted like some kind of a demon god is sitting on a throne in a first class hotel such as the Waldorf Astoria in New York. Only the face is of the Kabuki. The rest of him is dressed in a conservative business suit. He is reverently chanting to a picture of a Buddhist temple with a dollar sign prominently displayed. The chant is "money om" which he nasally repeats over and over, faster and faster, until he is interrupted by a phone call. He answers.

REV MONEY

REV. MONEY speaking. Oh hallelujah! It's my favorite stockbroker, ROLLO PIPPICK. Yes, I'm glad you called. The Church of Money has many orders to place today. I want you to buy all available media shares... Don't worry! I'm sending you a check for a trillion dollars... I got it for nothing selling candy, flowers and Korean sushi to the suckers... I'm tired of being slandered by Satan's lies... If you can't fool the media, you have to buy it... That's the American way stupid. And see if you can pick up Yankee Stadium too... I need it for my mass marriages of course. And I have nice Korean Christian girl for you... You're Jewish! (Almost barfs) So sorry, I must have ate too much Kimchi for breakfast. And don't forget my Hershey chocolate takeover... (Furious) What do you mean I got all the candy I need? We've got to have Hershey. It's important for our all American image... Of course candy is a spiritual blessing. Candy is better than yin and yang...

Buddhist heresy my kimchi wok! They've got a few winners like you can't believe. I'm even thinking of taking over the chanting market from the Hare Krishna wackos... I can't rip off their chant because it's a pagan chant and we're some kind of pseudo wacko Christian Messiah conglomerate... Sure their chant is profitable. They take in eighty million a month... Pennies from heaven are pennies earned... Eh! I have a great chant we can capitalize for a hundred billion the first year... Of course we will vibrate better than other religions. Money Om! It's the money vibration of the universe... Hold on to those primal scream stock options. I've got a hot insider tip for you. I'm starting a Society of Screaming for the Propagation of Fire and Brimstone Preaching... No! Sexual therapy groups are bad business for white bread Christians... Because it makes them headstrong and virile and you have to give them a cold shower before you brainwash them. That's why I have my followers sell candy. It ruins virility and everybody has to buy my Ginseng to regain his health... If you don't like candy, don't tell anybody you're my stockbroker... Bless you too Mr. Penis with a small P. (Bangs down phone) Well, you can't expect every Christ killer to become good Money child over night. (He resumes chanting and after the first few "money oms" the doorbell rings.) Now who in the name of Satan is that? I left strict orders that I wasn't to be disturbed. (Bell rings again) Come in!

A very pretty girl enters. REV. MONEY jumps off the throne and assumes a defensive Tae Kwon Do position. When the girl reaches into her pocketbook, Rev. Money anticipating an assassination attempt runs and hides behind his large throne. FANNY MARTIN takes REV. MONEY effigy candle from her purse that she had intended to present to REV. MONEY, but when he disappears, she places the candle on a step of the throne, lights it and genuflects to it in the Mohammedan way of praying. After MONEY recovers from his fright, he cautiously approaches her from her vulnerably exposed rear angle.

                REV. MONEY
What is the meaning of your barging into the FATHER'S private sanctuary and startling me his number one throne warmer? And stop praying to that idolatrous candle.

                FANNY MARTIN
I have brought the father an offering.

                REV. MONEY
Candles are not part of the ritual of the Church of Money.

                FANNY
They should be. Think of the money the church could make selling wax effigies of the FATHER, like this one.

                REV. MONEY
We have banned candles because they are not perishable enough to make a profitable sale each and every minute. Some of them last for months and months.

                FANNY
This candle has built in instant obsolescence. It can only be used one time, because the wick is only long enough to burn for one minute. I got a great promotional jingle to go with it. Listen up! But wait, I can't speak to you. I've got to speak to the FATHER, personally.

                REV. MONEY
You don't recognize me? I am the REV.

MONEY. I have my face on all the newspapers; I'm on T.V. each and every night, and my posters are everywhere or were until that red menace SATAN made me take them down. Now out with that jingle. I may be able to use it.

                    FANNY

You sure you can't show me some I.D.? You're a little less than what I expected in person. I thought you'd be more of a super star type. You know how they paint their faces crazy (His is crazy) and wear outrageous clothes to impress the teenyboppers?

                    REV. MONEY

(Takes a letter out of pocket) Take a look at this endorsement. What better credentials could I have than this letter signed by Him? (Pointing skyward)

                    FANNY

(Handing back) This letter could be a forgery.

                    REV. MONEY

A forgery! Out young lady. I will not ask the LORD to verify his signature for you or anyone else. Out! Before I call my guards and they aren't as kind as I am and will probably heave you right out the window making you into an instant Money angel.

                    FANNY

I'm sorry I doubted you FATHER. Please try to understand that I was taking these precautions for your benefit. Now listen to this. A candle at nine is divine. A candle at ten is your friend. A candle at eleven is heaven. So don't be in the dark at twelve or you may end up in hell. Buy Rev. Money effigy candles and be saved from eternal darkness. All money to be donated by the Church of Money to the Lighthouse for the Morally Blind. A subsidiary of the Church of Money, of course.

REV. MONEY
I like part of your idea young lady, but quite frankly, I have more money than I need right now. What really concerns me at the moment is my image. Got any ideas?

FANNY
I have ideas unlimited. If I could do a few things to give you a better looking throne room, then we could have endless followers.

REV. MONEY
What do you mean we, white girl?

FANNY
I mean you and I. The two of us together will form a partnership in the Money business.

REV. MONEY
My child! You have very enlarged gall stone of brain and halitosis of ego coming here and putting this proposition to me MONEY about you and I going into partnership in the money business...
Who are you my dear?

FANNY
I'm someone who wants to help you. I want to help myself. I hear you are going to save America from SATAN?

REV. MONEY
You better Hong Kong Pusan believe it my child.

FANNY
I want to be on the winning side. I want to play on the winning team. You're on Gods' side, right?

REV. MONEY
Right!

FANNY
Well last time I was on SATAN'S side and it didn't work out that well.

MONEY
You worked for SATAN? Abomination! Aveck! Aveck!

FANNY
Cool it!

MONEY
Aveck! Aveck!

FANNY
Aveck? What language is that?

MONEY
Yiddish. And it means you go straight to hell, because you stink, of sulfurous damnation.

FANNY

It's only vintage Channel #5 and besides
where did you learn to speak Yiddish?

     MONEY

From my stockbroker ROLLO PENIS.

     FANNY

Yiddish? Well, I'll tell ya honey, I
mean MONEY, SATAN didn't pay as well as
I think God will pay. Am I right?

     MONEY

God pays off in spades.

     FANNY

I prefer money, but a well-hung spade
    will do in a pinch.

     MONEY

You have very sick mind. Must go to
pollution control center and wash body
mind and soul until turn into goodie
two shoes.

     FANNY

Yes FATHER. I can't wait to have a mental
douche. I'll be going now.

     MONEY

That's right my girl. But just a minute!
Before you are so kind as to split from my
divine presence, would you please explain to me how you, a frail insignificant
female, were able to come through my
temple gates, past my humongous body builders, through the forest of booby traps,
over the barbed wire, past the submachine guns,
over the top of balcony covered with
broken glass, down stairway past four Tae
Kwon Do experts and make your entrance

completely unscathed into my private
throne room here at the Waldorf Astoria
hotel?

          FANNY

There are no barriers before a seductive
women. Especially when she's walking
past men who haven't had the courage or
wit to touch a woman in a millennium.
All they could do was stand at attention
and gape.

          MONEY

Are you talking dirty?

          FANNY

I said gape, not rape. Besides they
wouldn't know what to do with it and I
bet you wouldn't either.

          MONEY

Now wait a minute. You think I am the
Messiah who must create the new master
race and I don't know what to do with it?
Is this what you are saying?

          FANNY

Can you prove otherwise?

          MONEY

My dear, I'm a virgin. That's the main
part of our creed.

          FANNY

I wouldn't be proud of it.

          MONEY

I'm very proud of it.

FANNY
Why

MONEY
Because God is virgin.

FANNY
God is a virgin?

MONEY
He's not a virgin?

FANNY
Is that part of your rhetoric?

MONEY
Ah so, round eye.

FANNY
I think you're confusing the word virgin with happy. Since we are made in Gods image, he must be made in our image. And since most of us would rather be happy than be virgins, I think God is happy not to be an unhappy virgin. Got it! Perhaps you don't understand the English language too well. Maybe I could help you there too...

MONEY
Well. I must admit my English is a little Chung cho si ghi. That's ass backwards in French.

FANNY
Well, I could also help you with your French...

MONEY
No! No!

FANNY
With your Greek?

MONEY
No! I'm not interested in any French jobs or Greek jobs. I'm only interested in what you can do for me in English.

FANNY
In English?

MONEY
Yes.

FANNY
All right then. There is one universal language and you know what that is?

MONEY
Yes. God is love.

FANNY
Money.

MONEY
Money. Eh huh. Right! God is money.

FANNY
Money talks.

MONEY
Money talks, honey buckets walk.

FANNY
Now you're money.

MONEY
Right

FANNY
Now you're talking, but nobodies listening.

MONEY
Right... Huh? What' a ya mean?

FANNY
Now, why is nobody listening? Perhaps
because you're talking in Korean half
the time.

MONEY
You think that has something to do with
it?

FANNY
That has a lot to do with it. Especially
since you're here in the United States.
But don't worry. I can help you gain
vast numbers of followers who before this
would have thought you were another one
of those imported charlatans...

MONEY
No! Kuro chi! Asunida! Falsehood!
Liar! Kojimal! Anti-Christ! I don't
want to hear it. I am the true Messiah.
I am God's messenger on earth. On
Easter Sunday 1936, I had a vision on a
hillside in Korea where Jesus himself
told me to carry out his unfulfilled task
of marrying and spawning the master race.
My mission is to save America, which is
going to hell from all the crime, alcohol-
ism, divorce, drug abuse, sex and subversive Satanism. God has sent me here to
solve all of these problems and to mobilize
an ideological army of young people to
unite the world in a new age of truth.
All obstacles to God's truth must be
annihilated from the face of the earth.
Then there will be peace in this land and
my word will be law, because I am the

bullet of God.

FANNY
Cool it! Cool it!

MONEY
What?

FANNY
You don't sell anything like that.

MONEY
You don't. That's how we do it in Korea.

FANNY
No. You don't sell things like that.
You have to be sort of sophisticated.
You have to get to people when they least
expect it. You have to be there
subliminally.

MONEY
Sub what? What does that mean?

FANNY
Subliminally. It means, for example, if
you had your face on every sheet of toilet
paper in this country, you'd be there...
you know... every time somebody had to go
to the bathroom, you'd be there. They'd
think of you. You'd be on their minds.

MONEY
No! I'd be on their asses.

FANNY
Well, any attention is better than none.

MONEY
I hadn't thought of it like that.

FANNY
I mean you have to saturate.

MONEY
Every bathroom in the country with toilet paper with my face on it?

FANNY
You got your kids selling candy. Why not toilet paper? Why not a million other things?

MONEY
Like what?

FANNY
Ahh...

MONEY
We already have it. We already have a corner on the corner of 33rd and Eighth Ave, a corner on the sushi market, the ginseng market and the candy market and we're trying to take over the chanting market from the screw balls.

FANNY
Forget chanting. What you could use is a hit song. Number one with a bullet.

MONEY
I already am a bullet and I have a hit song. Listen.

(Sings) My name is Rev. Money
    I am the new Messiah
    Did someone call me liah
    Get on your knees and pray
    Hooray, hooray, hooray
    I come from South Korea

> To preach that God is dandy
> And save the world with candy
> Hooray, hooray, hooray.
> Get on your knees and pray

And on the flip side is!

> Ask any Moonie
> You happen to see
> Tuna packed in Ginseng
> Is Kosher with me.

FANNY
Who writes them?

MONEY
I do.

FANNY
You're not going to have a hit in this country with an old Marx Bro's tune and an advertising jingle. You need to rap or have a good pogo beat. You need to be on target FATHER.

MONEY
You do?

FANNY
Yeah! You're not playing small time sandlot baseball anymore. You got 'a go around, touch all the bases and score.

MONEY
Now just a minute. Before you start talking about scoring, let's get something very straight.

FANNY
Oh! (Innocently) Was I talking about

scoring?

MONEY
Yes you were. And in my organization, huggy body, kissee facee, but no touchee pee pee... It's the creed of the movement.

FANNY
What a dull existence. How do you expect your followers to multiply if you don't, shall we say, let them have sexual intercourse?

MONEY
Members of my church become eligible for sexual intercourse only after they have faithfully served the movement for seven years. Even then they need my personal approval for marriage. They may propose a mate of their own choice, but ultimately I make the final decision on who marries whom. They may then know each other in the biblical sense, but only on Wednesdays and only after they have fasted all day. That's the only time they can do it.

FANNY
Don't you let them have any fun?

MONEY
Fun? Fun! I am pure and purity is something like a blossom before it is open. Before you are blessed, you must keep the blossom shut tight and bear the fragrance deep within you. I myself remain chaste, pure and concentrate my energies on making money.

FANNY
But don't you understand there are many

ways of having fun that don't involve
making money?

MONEY
Unless you are making money, there is no
way of having fun.

FANNY
Don't knock it if you haven't tried it.

MONEY
I haven't tried it and if I knocked it
up I wouldn't confess to it anyway.

FANNY
Well, wouldn't it be a great idea if we
got all your followers together. Just
think of it. You could marry them. Two
million of them. You could have one
mass (Pun) ceremoney. Do you like that?
You could have it covered by the press.
They could all lose their virginity at
the same time. Two million people.

MONEY
That'd be an awful lot of dirty laundry.

FANNY
Well, that's where the REV. MONEY condoms
come in. Keeps everything neat.

MONEY
My what?

FANNY
REV. MONEY condoms with your picture on
the side of every box.

MONEY
How about on the side of every condom?

FANNY
Maybe on the end. So that your smile
would stretch. You'd be right there to
bless every fuck.

MONEY
Wow! What an idea. REV. MONEY condoms
with my smile on the end of them so that
when you're fornicating you're getting
fornicated by REV. MONEY, out front.

FANNY
I'd call that in deep.

MONEY
You do have a way with words, young lady.
Tell me. What did you do before you
decided to come here and become a member
of my organization?

FANNY
Well, I have a PhD in psychology and I've
been doing market research for some of
the biggies...

MONEY
What do you mean biggies? Who's bigger
than REV. MONEY? And I've never heard
of you.

FANNY
You've heard of Michael Jackson?

MONEY
Another fraud.

FANNY
Another fraud? You know how much
money he made? He made so much

money, he could afford to retire at the
age of fifteen. How does that sound?

            MONEY
Not bad. I'm 26 and still struggling.

            FANNY
Well don't admit it. You should be
ageless to your followers.

            REV. MONEY
Spectacular idea.

            FANNY
That's only one of my ideas. You've
heard of the skate board and the tickle
me doll? Well those were my ideas too.

            MONEY
They were. What did you say your name is?

            FANNY
I'm FANNY MARTIN and I'm the world's
number one promoter. I take mediocre
nonentities like you and I make them into
bigger mediocre non-entities so that
everyone in the nation identifies and
imitates. And there is a lot of money
to be made. For both of us.

            MONEY
Now wait a minute. Did you say for both
     of us?

            FANNY
I said for both of us.

            MONEY
No, no, no. I run this church! If you
want to come in and work with us, I think

there might be a small insignificant
candle promoting position open. However,
if you're thinking of starting at the top
young lady, I think you have another
think coming.

          FANNY
If I don't start at the top, in six
months there isn't going to be any top
or any bottom or any middle to this
organization. (She sits on his throne)

          MONEY
(Yanks her off throne infuriated) There
can be only one person who sits at the
top of the pyramid and I am that person.

          FANNY
(Furious) You can sit there if you like
and I can see you like it. You can have
the throne FATHER, but if you want to
become the GARTH BROOKS or MICHAEL
JACKSON of Messiah's you better let me
handle the money. And I don't mean you!

          MONEY
I wasn't offering myself.

          FANNY
Good.

          MONEY
All right. You got the number two spot.
I love your ideas about making money.
I like several of your promotional ideas.
Sort of. But there are certain precepts
within this organization which must be
established forever without changing,
because they come directly from above
wherein my whole scam is built. Now, at

the top of the list. No pre-marital
sex at all. Don't even think about it.
Next. Total devotion to the devious
policy of divine deception whereby we will
strip SATAN of his SATANIC money by any
means. All money is evil that doesn't
belong to MONEY. And most important of
all, total devotion to me, because I sit
at the top and everybody's got to stick
with me, because I am the divine glue
that holds all things in their natural
unified orbit. Those have got to be the
ground rules. None of the things you
come up with can alter that. Got it?

     FANNY
I've got it. You can have it. You can
keep it. You can shove it. I'm out 'a here.

     MONEY
Where you going?

     FANNY
I'm going to find another Messiah. One
who knows good advice when he hears it.

     MONEY
Just a minute FANNY FANNY.

     FANNY
Aha! You've been practicing your English
haven't you?

     MONEY
Come back here and let's discuss the fine
print. Perhaps we can have a meeting
of the minds.

     FANNY
That's a good place to start, but I hope

we can go on from there.

          MONEY

What do you mean? Everything is mind. The body is dirty dirty dirty.

          FANNY

I think if you go into the bathroom you can find a bar of soap.

          MONEY

Yes?

          FANNY

And if you go into the bedroom, you can find a bed.

          MONEY

Yes?

          FANNY

Why don't we go talk about it in more comfortable surroundings.

          MONEY

On a bar of soap?

          FANNY

In bed! With some tea for me, two oysters for you, some cookies for me. A more intimate tête-à-tête.

          MONEY

Are you talking dirty? If it's dirty, I can't do it.

          FANNY

It's only dirty if you do it in French. We'll do it in English.

MONEY
My English is very bad. Can we do it in
    Korean.

FANNY
I'm here to give you instruction in all areas in
    which you need instruction.

MONEY.
Oh no my dear. I'm here to give you instruction on how to be a virgin for Money's
    Angel Airline.

FANNY
Yes FATHER. I've always wanted to be
    flown enough to be a virgin angel.

CURTAINS SCENE 1/SCENE 2

MONEY is sitting on his throne reading the wall street journal.
He becomes progressively more upset and finally lets out a blood-curdling scream. This is the cue for FANNY MARTIN to make her entrance dressed in the traditional Korean costume. She is carrying a tea service that she places on a table near the throne. She shuffles mincingly across the room with head bowed in the characteristically submissive posture of a typical oriental housewife. After poring MONEY a cup of tea, she kneels and assumes a sort of Mohammedan praying position in front of MONEY. She begins to chant "money om" as the REVEREND is reading and mumbling "blasphemy" about what he is reading. When he finally speaks, he vents his frustrations on FANNY.

MONEY
Blasphemous sons of SATAN... Aw
shad up that vibrating women. You give
me the Holy Roller twitchees and I can't
even cuss right. Sulfurous damnation, inter-

course, goat feces. You know what seven
forked tongued communist Satin the Wall
Street Journal says about me? I claim to be
God and I am trying to corner the sardine
market. I need sardines for my Kimchi,
but I don't need the whole corner. When
everyone in the world eats my Kimchi,
there will be no more rapes and there'll be
a great market for my expensive designer
gas masks. I'm not God, I'm only... I
don't even claim to be. Maybe every other
Wednesday I claim to be, but that's just for
P.R. purposes. Nevertheless I fill all the
qualifications. Right! I got two eyes, two
hands, two feet, two faces, two of everything.
That's just what it says in the bible. And
most of all, I'm prime choice circumcised
male.

    FANNY
The new Messiah could be a woman.
Don't forget that... You're not a woman are
you?

    MONEY
Nah, I'm not a woman. Who says God
could be a woman?

    FANNY
I've heard it said.

    MONEY
By whom?

    FANNY
By feminists... of which I'm not one.

    MONEY
I'm glad you said that.

FANNY
Not me! I just repeat their evil gossip.

MONEY
What do you repeat their evil gossip for?

FANNY
You should know what's going on.

MONEY
What do you mean I should know what's going on. I read the newspapers. I see what's going on. I mean... I even own a bunch of newspapers.

FANNY
Half the people in the world are woman. You have to appeal to them too.

MONEY
Feces, urine, brimstone and corruption woman, pore me some more tea. I did in my last major appearance try to endear myself to women. I said be as like little children. I'm not too sure myself what I meant by that, but it certainly should have flattered women who love spending all their time being completely irresponsible demons, just like children. You know number two what's wrong with you American women? You're not submissive enough.

FANNY
We want to be, but it's just that American men don't have the balls to keep us in our places on our backs where we belong.

MONEY
That's a very sinful thing to say.

FANNY
I can't say that I've sinned personally, but um-American men leave a lot to be desired. It's Korean men I'm curious about.

MONEY
Yes, of course. (Slurping tea) Well um, Korean men get their virility, their strength and their wisdom from drinking this particular kind of tea.

FANNY
Oh! What kind of tea is that?

MONEY
This is Ginseng tea. I have a monopoly on all the Ginseng that comes out of Korea. It's great stuff. That's why Koreans are all kind, above board, true-blue and we hate SATAN and love GOD; all because we drink Ginseng tea... Here, try some...

FANNY
(Drinks) Oh... it has a sexy flavor.

MONEY
(Innocently) It is the radioactive yang that gives it the flavor.

FANNY
That yang is powerful stuff. I'm getting turned on.

FANNY now pretends to be as turned on as a cat in heat or one O.D.'ing on catnip. She rubs against MONEY'S legs and then rolls around on the floor purring in ecstasy as MONEY rather guiltily and nervously expounds on the tea's unique properties.

MONEY
Well it ah... it has many very powerful

properties. It contains a great deal of the cosmic element yin... no yang in oppostion to the feminine, which is yin. Everything in the world is a little unbalanced yin and yang because male must dominate. And this tea is yang chuck full. Right? It's better than a shot of testosterone.

          FANNY
(FANNY comes out of sexual reverie and becomes the promoter again)
Chuck full of yang! What a great gimmick.

          MONEY
Yeah!

          FANNY
Chuck full of yang. Wow!

          MONEY
Yeah. Chock full of yang.

          FANNY
Chuck full of yang. We'll put it on shelves coast to coast.

          MONEY
Sure!

          FANNY
Chuck full of yang. It'll cure baldness...

          MONEY
Yeah. Chuck full of yang. It'll even put hair on the chest of gays, women and other SATAN worshipers. Another great idea from the Church of Money.

FANNY
What do you mean? That was my idea.

MONEY
You extracted if from my cosmic consciousness on which I have a patent pending.

FANNY
That's your idea?

MONEY
Right!

FANNY
It's all your idea? What about Shirley Mc what's-her-name?

MONEY
(Cuts her off) Everything is all my idea. Now you're cooking. Let me tell you something else about this yang stuff. Fabulous. You drink this tea and it comes into your system and suddenly you get a swelling and a purifying and you start to sweat and your hair grows longer and you get big muscles... and it's really good for all your organs... I mean especially your reproductive organs. You ought a see the... I mean those Koreans man drink this tea by the gallon and they got schlongs that you could fill a Jewish deli sandwich with. It's tremendous stuff. It's fabulous. Why...

FANNY
Oh my goodness! How would you know FATHER?

MONEY
Why, I'm Korean, I drink a barrel a day and I got the biggest schlong on the block.

FANNY
Are you going to show me?

MONEY
I will not show you my large reproductive organ, but you can drink this tea and I guarantee all your reproductive organs will be really snappy. You my little virgin will not develop a big schlong, but you'll develop swell breasts and there's nothing wrong with your breasts even though breasts are an abomination in the eyes of the lord. (Money has fingers just inches from FANNY'S breasts that are thrust toward him temptingly) And I must always remember our eleventh commandment. No touchee titty titty.

FANNY
(Who still acts like she's had an overdose of catnip.)
FATHER?

MONEY
Yes?

FANNY
I have a confession to make.

MONEY
You have. Go ahead and confess my child.

FANNY
I lied to you when I told you I was a

virgin.

MONEY
Good. You're learning fast. Lying is our fourteenth commandment. I in fact lied to you when I told you us Koreans have large schlongs. Go ahead...

FANNY
You mean you're not upset.

MONEY
With what? My big schlong?

FANNY
Why I... I thought you'd be upset when I told you I'm not a virgin.

MONEY
You're not a virgin?

FANNY
That's what I said.

MONEY
I didn't hear you. I was preoccupied with my expanded... consciousness...

FANNY
(Looking close) Oh... I see...

MONEY
Whadaya mean you're not a virgin?

FANNY
Well... before I was converted by you FATHER, I spent a good many years being a nymphomaniac psychologist.

MONEY
Is that someone who directs traffic?

FANNY
No... Unless you want to consider men in and out of your bedroom as traffic.

MONEY
Oooooooooooh!

FANNY
It sometimes gets to be a bit of a hassle when your second lover...

MONEY
Oh my...

FANNY
... comes in before the first one leaves.

MONEY
Great sulfurous fumes of Hades! You have more than one man a night? It's bad enough you should sin, but twice a night?

FANNY
But listen. How can it be sin if I give it away? And I keep the first man from being selfish. After all, there's more than enough of me to go around. And I'm getting something too, aren't I?

MONEY
Are you?

FANNY
A little here, a little there...

MONEY
You're getting laid a lot is what you're getting. I mean that's just terrible. That's cardinal and you weren't even taking yang.

FANNY
I was doing a survey of schlongs.

MONEY
You were? Really?

FANNY
Really. I wanted to see whether men who have big schlongs were any better lovers than men who didn't have big schlongs. And my conclusions were all men can be great lovers. All men can be great lovers if they have a wonderful sensuous women to guide them into the pleasures in the realms of the senses. I don't think men should have to pay for sex. I like to give it away.

MONEY
You do?

FANNY
Yeah.

MONEY
That's dumb. That's really dumb.

FANNY
You think I should get something for it?

MONEY
Sure! Two bucks a head. Two guys a night. That's... No, no, no, no... That's an abomination. No good. No good. That's

a terrible thing my child. How did you
ever develop this craving for men? What
is that all about? I do not understand.

FANNY

I thought that I was doing some good
works, some charitable deeds by giving
men the opportunity to sample the joys
of my body without having to pay for it.
Without having to commit themselves to
a loveless marriage.

MONEY

Just a minute. Wait a minute. I don't
understand. People get married. I mean
that's the whole point. That you legi-
tamize the nooky-nooky. Is that not
correct? Why do you give it away for
nothing?

FANNY

I couldn't marry all the men who wanted
me.

MONEY

No. That's true. You couldn't. But
why so many? I don't understand why so
many?

FANNY

Well, Baskin-Robbins has 31 flavors.

MONEY

Yes.

FANNY

I like to try all the flavors. It's the
same thing with men. But there are so
many...

MONEY
Do you mean... there are some men like
banana and whipped cream... and there
are other men that are like tutti-frutti
ice cream and then... my favorite is black
cherry. No never mind... Go ahead...

FANNY
Most of them are a little nutty really.
Like pistachio.

REV. MONEY
There are pistachio men?

FANNY
There are pistachio men, there are almond...

MONEY
Almond men?

FANNY
Walnut men...

MONEY
Walnut?

FANNY
Very tasty... Walnut men...

MONEY
Strangest thing I ever have heard. Walnut
men! Have you ever had a Korean?

FANNY
I've never had a Korean.

MONEY
Then you don't know what a Korean tastes
like?

FANNY
No, no... But, I figure they taste somewhere between um Octopus testicles and coconut milk with a little monkey brains thrown in for seasoning.

MONEY
That's the strangest... Wow! Hummmm... My goodness. I don't know anything about this strange ice cream. This is remarkable. Maybe I should take over the ice cream market and sell Michael Jordan flavored ice cream.

FANNY
I'm still looking for a man who tastes like bubble gum.

MONEY
Bubble gum?

FANNY
Bubble gum! That's another idea. We can have REV. MONEY bubble gum.

MONEY
And put it on men's penises?

FANNY
Yeah. You know. I think you've come up with something really big. We can have REV. MONEY bubble gum condoms.

MONEY
REV. MONEY bubble gum condoms?

FANNY
Yeah. We can make them in 31 flavors

just like Baskin-Robbins. We can sell
them in candy stores and motels coast to
coast. We'll put vending machines in
subways and on street corners everywhere.
We'll clean up in Times Square. We'll
get endorsements from everyone from
Madonna to Dennis Rodman. That's not all.
We can sell franchises. Move over Col.
Sanders. Why settle for finger licking
good when you can go all the way with
REV. MONEY. The family that chews together screws together. Double your
blessedness double your fun, the day of
the bubble gum condom has come. REV.
MONEY bubble gum condoms. A flavor for
every day of the month.

     MONEY
Do people fornicate that often?

     FANNY
You mustn't think like that.

     MONEY
No, you're right. That's dirty, dirty,
dirty. Don't think like that. No, no, no!

     FANNY
I'm thinking of MONEY. REV. MONEY bubble
gum condoms. They come in thirty-one
flavors.

     MONEY
You're a very sick girl. Come and continue your confessions. I must hear it
all even if I pee my pants in 31 flavors.

     FANNY
I'm just trying to help.

MONEY
Yeah. Thank you my dear. Now, you've
told me that you gave yourself up to men
so that they could sample you as a sort of
non-religious church like scientology.
But even scientology charges thousands.
Why do you give your charity for free?

FANNY
Why?

MONEY
Yes.

FANNY
Ooh... Why, it's one of life's great
pleasures to experience other people.

MONEY
You have to experience them in bed?

FANNY
Well... Most men, you can't talk to them,
but you can ball them... Can you understand that?

MONEY
No. Uh uh.

FANNY
Do you know how hard it is for a woman
like me with a PhD in psychology to find
men that I can talk to? But if I ball
them first and then find the ones I like,
then I can decide whom I want to talk to.
Doesn't that make sense?

MONEY
You know, now that you put it that way,

you might have something there.

          FANNY
I had a lot actually.

          MONEY
Yes, I bet you did.

          FANNY
But I've given it all up for you.

          MONEY
You have?

          FANNY
That's why I'm telling you this all now, because it's all in the past.

          MONEY
Yes, I'm glad to hear that.

          FANNY
I don't want to give it away anymore.
I want to sell it for the cause.

          MONEY
Well yes. But wait a minute. I don't
think you have that idea quite correctly.
It's good that you're saving it now.
And it is good that all of that is in
the past. Nevertheless, you must realize
that the entire Church is based on no
fornication before marriage.

          FANNY
Will you marry me?

          MONEY
I think I must humbly decli...

                                FANNY
                Will you impregnate me so that I may give
                birth to the master race of Messiahs
                that will save the world from SATAN?

                                MONEY
                Is that anything like getting married?

                                FANNY
                No.

                                MONEY
                Then I won't do it. I think you've con-
                fessed enough for today. As for myself,
                I'm going out and have a double shot of holy
                water to wash out my mind.
                (Exits)

                                FANNY
                We won't know if this man is God until
                he has really been tempted.

CURTAIN SCENE II/CURTAIN SCENE III

REV. MONEY enters his throne room alone and seats himself on his throne. The throne turns into a sort of desk with a food tray attached to it that he unfolds and on which he opens a laptop computer and begins to work.

                                MONEY
                Hurry up women. She's a real fanatic.
                I can't get her away from the candle
                assembly line long enough to drink a cup
                of Ginseng assembly line tea. Praise
                be to Jesus computers are going to replace
                women in the new scheme of things. (Phone
                rings) Billy Crackers. How are you? It's
                so nice to hear your voice again. It
                seems like a millennium... Yes indeed.

We've come a long way since those Korean War crusades. Thanks to you SATAN is still up on the thirty-eighth parallel eating his heart out... What do you mean I'm infringing on your turf? I figure one good turn deserves another. SATAN has been putting you out of business because you haven't modernized your hype. You need to be more sophisticated, more (mispronounced subliminal) sublerminal than 45 years ago. Sublerminal? Why, it means you have to be hidden everywhere like a germ. Just think how big you would be if we put your germ in Penicillin. Me bananas. Oh, you can't believe what you read in the newspapers. They just love to malign and castigate the helpless. Especially the president. The media is completely under the control of SATAN. You know what they did to me when I spoke at Yankee stadium. Falsified the weather reports. They predicted tornadoes in the area. The only tornadoes they've ever had in that area are the hooligans. It's a good thing I rescinded turn the other cheek instructions and authorized my Tornado Trooper brigade to hand out God blessed Karate chops to those mother's of abomination free of charge... How's life in Hicksville BILLY??? You think you may be the Messiah BILLY? Listen BILLY ole buddy, I think you're a nice cracker, but the Messiah can't be a Caucasian again... BILLY, I have the greatest respect for your rhetoric so don't force me to devastate you in a debate over the advantages of slant eyes verse round eyes. O.K.? Give my best regards to SATAN BILLY. Oh you quit smoking? Bye bye BILLY. Who needs

him? And the nerve of that phony...
Thinks he's God and he's got one foot
in redneck hick country and the other in
hell. In the sulfurous name of BILLY
CRACKERS woman where are you?

          FANNY
(Entering hastily) I'm sorry FATHER. I
just finished the final draft on your
press release announcing our Super Save
America from SATAN Sexaid.

          MONEY
My English... What's a sexaid?

          FANNY
It's kind of a big blooper like
those crusades in the Middle Ages. And
believe me, there's nothing like a big
blooper to make a big publicity splash.

          MONEY
We will make bloopers our twelfth
commandment and clean up selling
indulgences.

          FANNY
Right. REV. MONEY sexaid bloopers. Two
for the price of one.

          MONEY
No. No sex. I think you better change
the word sexaid to crusade or you may
need first aid.

          FANNY
That's it. A Super Save America from
SATAN first aid Crusade.

MONEY
Now you're cooking. In this age of mass
communication madness, I am not yet
big enough to cast my bloopers before
the swine. Got it number two?

FANNY
Sorry FATHER. It was an honest blooper.

MONEY
One more mistake number two and I'll
have you crucified by your nose ring,
the penalty if I lose face. Now, let me
hear that press release and it better be hymenal.
(Another blooper. He meant hymnal) I
love to hear them sung.

FANNY
A hymnal? Of course my infallible
FATHER. (Tries to sing like a hymn) The
Church of Money and it's founder the REV.
MOON SUN MONEY are happy to announce
that the greatest crusade in the history of the
world will take place in America to honor
the birth of the greatest SATAN buster
in the history of this nation and to
dedicate a statute of him at the top of
Mt. Teton. REV. MOON SUN MONEY will
personally lead the march of two million
born again Church of Money MONEY-
CHILDREN from New York City to
Grand Teton, Wyoming. Upon reaching
Mt. Teton, there will be twenty-four hours
of ceremoneys beginning with a marathon
dedication speech by REV. MONEY, after
which will come a fireworks display that
will put MONEY in the sky all the way
around the world. Last but not least, this
great crusade will climax with the greatest

climax in the history of the world, when
the REV. MONEY marries in one mass ceremoney two million people. The REV.
MONEY will then personally endorse each
fuck thus guaranteeing to the world a new
master race of people completely immune
to the temptations of SATAN. A-men.

              MONEY
Perfect! Perfect! A beautiful hymenal.
You're a genius my dear. Sit down right
here on the throne just beneath me.

              FANNY
But where are we going to get one million
engaged couples?

              MONEY
Relax my love. Rest your pretty head.
It's all being arranged by computer. Any
one of my children is perfectly suited
for any other because they all agree
with me 100% to start with. They all
want to spend their lives hating
SATAN and selling my sushi candy bars.

              FANNY
I'm just worried about the logistics of
the whole thing. Don't you think that
people along the route will look upon
us as a plague of locust?

            REV. MONEY
Anyone that would look upon two million
perfectly groomed apple pie looking all-
American young people waving the flag and
singing Onward Money Soldiers as a plague
would be branded as a traitor to his
country and I would hope this SATAN wor-

shipper would be crucified on the
nearest cottonwood tree.

          FANNY
Sounds like you have been staying up late
watching old western movies FATHER.
But how are all these people going to eat
and perform other necessary functions?

          REV. MONEY
I shall perform even greater miracles
than any prophet in the history of the
world. Just wait until you see how many
port-a-johns I have flying through the
sky and we'll collect the honey from those
johns and re-cycle it into manna from
heaven granola bars. O.K. my child? If
I am the Messiah as is strongly suspected,
everything's gonna be O.K. Tell me number
two, when does the crusade begin?

          FANNY
If we start one week from today, we can
get there in time for the forth of July.

          MONEY
We bloodie well better, because I'm going
to give a rooten-tooten fireworks display
that'll remind the bloodie round eyes who
really invented bloodie fireworks. And
I think we should have the fireworks
before my dedication speech. After the
verbal pyrotechnics of my speech, who
would be so dull as to want to see real
fireworks? I don't like to see fifty million
samollians go up in smoke unless my
followers can have brains washed clean.
Clean brain is next to godliness, my
thirteenth commandment.

                    FANNY
But, FATHER. You have a captured
audience. Our two million faithful won't
leave until after the fireworks when you
will marry them. You can be certain of
one thing. As refined carbohydrate milksop
wasted as they are, they still got a firecracker
or two of their own they want to explode
when you legitimatize roman candles and
cherry bombs getting together and making
whoopie. But I think they should be
compelled to suffer thru the fireworks
last, as boring as it might be, because to
suffer is Christian and they should
make this one last gesture as proof
against SATAN'S hard to resist
temptations.

                    MONEY
That is some of the most disgustingly
stupid and vulgar imagery I have ever
heard, but you are right about making
them suffer. We shall make suffering
the fourteenth commandment. However,
listen to this women. Improve your
ideas and come up with some more imag-
inative promotions or I may have to
hire a real Madison Ave. pro to take your
place. Your ideas are old fashioned.
Douche out your dirty mind while I go
practice up on my new miracles.

REV. MONEY exists and FANNY who has been violently hurled to the floor bursts into a flood of crocodile tears. FANNY is not a bone fide cult slave. She is a feminist writer who has infiltrated the Church of Money to write an expose about its macho leader. For this reason the tears in the following speech are fake and interspersed with winks and other devices to let the audience in on the joke.

FANNY
He's so beautiful. Oh so gentle, so won-
derfully inscrutable. He's amazing grace
under fire. He's a walking miracle. And
I'm going to lose him. (Sniffle sniffle)
He's so righteous. He guarantees success
to all who follow him and obey his commands.
And several have become big name actors
and shakers too in spite of the number-
less losers who flock to him. This great
Korean Messiah is the new George Washington
No doubt about it. The country will once
again be sired and founded on the principal
that its leading men do not lie. He is so
honest that he has no idea how much money
he makes. And then everything is donated
to charity in spite of SATANS lies to the
contrary. (Bawls) And those horrible
lascivious politicians we send our vir-
ginal young people to help are such
demanding sinners. It is not enough we
have Big Mac parties for them, slip them
fat envelopes to instruct them how to
pass just and divine laws, but they swi-
zzle our Ginseng tea in such large quan-
tities that except for the FATHER'S
divine healing talent, there would not
be a virgin left in our flock. But we
persevere. The catalogue of our success
is mind warping. I wouldn't be surprised
if Korea doesn't become the 51st state.
(Cries hysterically) It's such good work
we MONEY children do and nobody understands
us except other cult slaves. (New excite-
ment of a promoter) But we shall soon
announce our new revelations and we shall
see who is God and who isn't God. (Like
a holy-roller turn on) Oh lord lord! I
can't tell you how almost sexually excited
I get when I think of our new revelations.

Jackseng Daniels. Can you imagine it?
The most vital herb in nature, God's own
medicine, combined with one of SATAN'S
most destructive temptations. Ginseng
Daniels. It'll remove rust from your reproductive organs. It will be like putting God
and SATAN in the same bottle. Naturally,
it will be a little GOD and a lot of SATAN,
but a little diluted GOD can defeat a
pure hard-boiled SATAN anytime. And
before we are finished we'll have it in
Cadillac Margaritas. Satan's favorite
is Scotch with bagpipe music. This is
the breath of the Loch Ness monster,
Satan's mother ship. No wonder the
Scotch are the most debauched dissenters
since the dripping driveling demented
damned were first invented by MARX in
the year of the devil 1848. It might also
have something to do with the bars closing at nine P.M. in Edinburgh. That's
hardly enough time for happy hour. Wow!
I'm so excited. Wait till you hear the rest.

MONEY
Come and pore me some tea number two. I
want to show you a fantastic new miracle.

FANNY
He doesn't hate me anymore. I'm so happy.
Coming master. (FANNY EXITS)

CURTAIN SCENE III/ CURTAIN SCENE IV

While the lights are down, there is the sound of grunting and puffing and heavy breathing, which easily could be confused with a couple having sex. When the lights come up again, the Reverend Money and FANNY MARTIN are seen to be facing each other dressed in black belt Tae Kwon Do uniforms doing breathing exercises. (Tae Kwon Do is the Korean version of Karate)

          MONEY
This kind of breathing is called Sumchigi. It means power gathering. If you do it properly you will be invincible.

          FANNY
Suppose your opponent also does it properly?

          MONEY
My technique is far superior to that of any mere mortal. Now, we come to the more physical part of the exercise. Do everything precisely as I do.

REV. MONEY goes thru a catalogue of Tae Kwon Do including bowing at beginning and end with the crossed arms ritual. FANNY does a mirror image of everything the REVEREND does

          MONEY
First bow with arms crossed thus. Then stand at attention called Cherriot. Next is Chumbi the ready stance. This Han-Dan Makgi is a low block. Next is the middle punch called Chong-kwon chigi. Counter this with Chang-Kwon chigi the famous palm strike. Now, step w/left foot & block W/left arm, table punch down w/rt arm, scrape punch uppercut w/rt. hand & swing left arm and foot back at same time, blocking with right arm. Bow at end.

          FANNY
(Fanny hits Moon) Sorry about that lucky punch FATHER.

REV. MONEY
You learn quickly my little number two
MONEY slave.

FANNY
No wonder. This is almost the same as
Karate. And I have a black belt.

MONEY
(Kicks her in bust) That is the difference.
Koreans are superior to Japs because
we kick.

FANNY
(Kicks him back) That's what I call fun.

MONEY
Where did you get black belt?

FANNY
Influence I guess. I had a deluded
patient once who thought he was a human
threshing machine. He would come in my
office waving his arms around and breaking everything and threatening me with
bodily harm. I found out he used to be
a black belt Karate expert. I decided to
take a few lessons so I could communicate
with him in Karate. I took Tae Kwon Do
by mistake and learned to kick. I had no
success with him until one day he made
me so mad he caused me to break a fingernail.
I was so infuriated that I kicked him in the
head so hard he flew right through a brick
wall and landed head first in a commode in
the ladies room shattering the commode and
causing three nervous breakdowns. I rushed

into the room expecting to see a bloodie
heap, but finding instead a smiling gentle
Japanese man bowing to me. He talked to me
lucidly for the first time. "Madame," he said,
"that was the best one legged hook I have
ever had the good fortune to block. That
low life Korean maneuver has failed again.
Who are you and may I please have your
autograph?" When I explained what he was
doing in my office, he apologized for
all the problems he had caused me, stated
he was cured, and offered to help me get
a black belt in Karate, which I soon did.

          MONEY
I think that's about the worst cock and
bull story I've ever heard.

MONEY now taunts FANNY with a whole bunch of quick punches and kicks her viciously before she is ready. A sort of Korean Pearl Harbor. FANNY counterattacks by grabbing MONEY by the wrist for leverage, turns and kicks him in the back of the head sending him flying to the floor.

          FANNY
I think that's the only patient I've
ever really cured.

          MONEY
You dirty sneaky little slut. I think it's
time I gave you a real lesson. You ready
to defend yourself against the only red
belt Tae Kwon Do expert in three hundred
years?

          FANNY
If you promise not to hurt me FATHER.

          MONEY
Every woman needs a kick once in a

while. It's my...

FANNY
...your nineteenth commandment I know.

MONEY
I promise you I could never hurt a woman.
These will be love taps.

FANNY
You promise on your mother's mustache?

MONEY
I promise on my father's beard that
hasn't been cut in a million light years.

FANNY and MONEY joust playfully in a circular movement with FANNY in the middle on the defensive. This is mostly thrusts and blocks that do no damage.

MONEY
Just as I thought. You're as incompetent
as a woman motorcycle cop. I eat tickets.

FANNY
It's just that I don't want to hurt a
Messiah with a warrant out on him.

MONEY
This is a waste of my fighting talent.
From now on number two your job will be
to wash dishes, scrub the floors and
nurse children.

FANNY
But you haven't even impregnated me yet.
Who am I going to nurse?

MONEY
We'll start you off with piglets. I have

some with human genes. The REV.
MONEY sausage turned out lousy, but
they suck titty big time.

                FANNY
But what about the master race? Are your
Moonchildren pigs? What about love?

                MONEY
Love is a word the weak use to subdue the
omnipotent. I'm going to annihilate you
as an object lesson to the weaker sex.
It is far better for women to be raped
than to foolishly try to defend themselves against men's superior strength
and wisdom. Always remember our forty-
ninth commandment. Women and children
should be seen and not heard.

                FANNY
Oh dear me FATHER. I feel so helpless
against this macho masculine logic. I
feel like such a creampuff. I can't wait
till you rape me and I produce the prototype
pig person for the master race. Come and get
it FATHER dearest. I'll gape and you rape.

MONEY lets out a ferocious shout and attacks for all he is worth. FANNY competently fends him off, but this is a real match with each side having to take it seriously to hold their own.

                MONEY
You see what I mean? You're nothing but
rape bait; a cheap lay FANNY FANNY.
A whore fit only for the comfort of our
Tornado Troopers.

FANNY finally loses her temper throwing caution to the wind and lets out an abdominal shout of incredible ferocity. Her attack onslaught leaves the REV. MONEY writhing on the ground in pain.

FANNY
(Remembering her mission)
Oh dear FATHER. I'm so sorry. I don't
know what came over me. But maybe
you'll come to your senses now and admit
that women can be equal to men. Are you
going to be O.K?

MONEY
Of course I'm O.K. How do you expect me
to teach you the proper submissive position
for a woman unless I sometimes pretend
I'm a stupid weak woman myself? Now
help me up. I'm anxious to get started on
our Super Save America from SATAN
Sexaid tomorrow. (Moans and groans
getting up) Oh...

FANNY
You made a real bloomer, I mean blooper,
I mean boo-boo this time FATHER. I
think you're going to need first aid to be
ready for that crusade tomorrow.

MONEY
I'll be O.K. I still have my Korean
cherry in tack.

FANNY
(Aside) Not for long.

CURTAIN SCENE IV/CURTAIN SCENE V

While the scene change is taking place from an interior throne room to an exterior road in Wyoming, there is a recording of Onward Money Soldiers playing. The mass march is within site of the Grand Tetons. The drop in the back could be two large mountain like breasts to add to the comic affect of the landscape. REV. MONEY & FANNY MARTIN are in hiking costume and enter singing Onward Money

Soldiers. He still retains the Kabuki face and wig as he does throughout the show. MONEY collapses soon after his entrance from fatigue and sore feet.

      MONEY
Oh oh oh! I don't think my divine feet
want to go any further. They're killing
me.

      FANNY
Let me massage your feet.

      MONEY
Ouch. Oh, oh! Be careful.

      FANNY
There. Does that feel better? Your
poor feet are all blistered.

      MONEY
No. It feels worse. How much further
is it? I thought it was just a days
march from N.Y.C. to Wyoming.

      FANNY
Look! We've almost made it. There's
the Grand Tetons in the distance, FATHER.
It's just a few more hours' march.

      MONEY
Help me up. We've got to circle the wagons
before an Indian raiding party.
spots us.

      FANNY
I think the sun has gone to his head.
The Indians are on our side, FATHER.
They're running our satellite communica-
tions station that will beam your Grand
Teton speech around the world.

MONEY
Oh, that's right. And Marlon Bluebonnet
is doing commercials for the Church.

FANNY
Yes, he and Dennis Rodchief are doing REV.
MONEY no friction guaranteed margarine
commercials for us.

MONEY
I thought one actor was suppose to be a
female?

FANNY
Well...

MONEY
Never mind. Help me up. I can't let those
boys go to all that work for nothing.

FANNY tries in every way to get MONEY to his feet with MONEY at one point falling on top of her, but all to no avail.

MONEY
Now that we have become a little more
intimate my dear, I think I have a confession to make. I suspect I am more
human than I thought I was. Why don't we
take a break. My divine feet don't give
a damn about those margarine commercials.
Besides my stomach tells me its time to
eat my China syndrome meltdown Kimchi.

FANNY
(Aside) Oh no. I'd rather be tied to
an anthill smelling his feet than eat
that Kimchi. (Trying to distract him)
FATHER, wouldn't you rather I read you
the latest news. (She pores newspapers
from her back pack)

MONEY
No! I'd rather make you eat some of my
national food Kimchi. (Pores Kimchi
from backpack)

FANNY
Oh please FATHER anything but that. I'd
rather eat the rattle on a rattlesnake
than that horrible smelling stuff.

MONEY
Eat!

FANNY
Please, I'm too young to die. And with
the holy mountain in sight. I never
thought we'd get this far.

MONEY
Eat!

FANNY
I'll die and my bones will bake here
in the desert forevermore.

MONEY
You'll be my Lazerous. I'll raise you
from the dead and be famous like Jesus.

FANNY
But Lazerous was a male and males are
easier to raise.

MONEY
My new miracles can raise women.

FANNY
That would be a miracle, but your miracles
are all a disaster so far. I don't

believe you. To hell with your miracles.

MONEY
(He tries to knock her down with his walking stick) Oh ye of little faith.

FANNY
You got that one right. You have to admit FATHER, your miracles have been less than a complete success. You know you almost drowned when you tried to walk across the Hudson.

MONEY
That is not a body of water. It's a body of filth belched up from the bowels of hell. I fainted from the stench when I was about half way across.

FANNY
That's what the New York Post said anyway.

MONEY
So did my other paper the Village Voice.

FANNY
The Paris Match called it a fraud and said you actually were walking on a tightrope hidden just below the surface of the water.

MONEY
That proves I'm not a tightrope walker. Besides who cares what those illiterate French think? Who speaks French except the French?

FANNY
And the Deutschland Ebnung News said that when you fell in the water, the pollution

level became so dangerously high, the
President of the U.S. called a press conference to announce that the government
would institute a crash program to eliminate MONEY pollution in the Hudson by
the year 2100.

MONEY
Those Nazi swine still haven't got any
human genes. Since the glorious days
of the third Reich, the Germans have
sunk to the pits of moral turpitude.

FANNY
And the Roma Pasta Gazette says you should
be crucified and burned alive and the
Italians would gladly take credit for it
this time.

MONEY
The Italians are a bunch of noodle thieves
who are getting ready to jump from SATAN'S
sauce pan right into the fires of hell.
Worst of all they think they're a bunch
of macho lovers. Well let me tell you
one thing. They made a big mistake when
they left Ginseng out of their tomato
sauce recipe. We Koreans can run
macho circles around them.

FANNY
And the Jerusalem Artichoke News says...

MONEY
I don't like vegetables. What about the
Arabs. I love their oil. I'm drilling
for it in my back yard in Beverly Hills.

FANNY
The Arab press isn't very friendly either.

The Saudi Arabian Harem News says if you
think you're going to replace Mohammed as
the true prophet spelled p-r-o-f-i-t,
they're going to start another oil embargo.

                MONEY
Those black hearted double-dealers. You
can't trust any Semitic. I'm going to have
our lobbyists in D.C. work for Iran. I
hear they are working on an anti-Semitic
flesh eating virus that attacks Arab
and Jewish noses with equal ferocity.

                FANNY
At least the American press has been
favorable. There is one little paper,
however, The Harpers Ferry Bulletin
that said your trying to feed two million
people with one net of fish from Lake
Michigan was a fishy flop.

                MONEY
That's some stupid queer in the woodpile
left wing rag that lies for the gaiety
of it. Can I help it if all the fish in
Lake Michigan are practicing sodomites
and are on strike against God?

                FANNY
What about Lazarous Goldstein who got
shot dead stealing a watermelon from a
farmers field. You promised to raise
him from the dead.

                MONEY
What do you want from me? He got to
heaven and found out it was a better deal
than this place of slings and arrows
of outrageous politicians and refused
to come back.

FANNY
And what about that awful poison ivy
epidemic that had everyone scratching so
hard the President of the U.S. had to
declare us a national disaster.

MONEY
Any fool can plainly see the President
of the U.S. is sometimes in bed with
SATAN. He vainly tries to be a prime
mover in all things. Before I had a
chance to effect a cure for the punishment
I had meted out for a premeditated pre-
marital petting incident, he had crop
dusters fly over the march and spray
our two million MONEY virgins with
Calamine Lotion. With do gooders like
that, we can hold our breath till hell
freezes over and there'll never be a
second coming. I will not stand for
a sanitized bug free world free of a
sensible amount of suffering. Everyone
should forget waterbeds and spend three days
a week sleeping on a bed of nails.

FANNY
Speaking of waterbeds. How about when you
ordered the Mississippi River to part
and allow the faithful to pass. We lost
almost one hundred thousand of the faithful
when they couldn't swim.

MONEY
They jumped my signal, but the waters finally
parted didn't they?

FANNY
I'm not sure. We cheated and walked across
a bridge. But the newspaper headlines said

you parted the waters so I guess it must
have happened. (She winks to audience and
holds up a copy of New York Times. Headline
says, "Money Parts Waters of Mississippi." A
headline just as big says paid advertisement)

            MONEY
We only walked across the bridge because
I had to set an example for the fools that
like to do things the hard way.

            FANNY
Then you announced you had found the
money frequency the universe vibrates to and
passed out vibrator business cards with
"Money Om" printed on them. You said
these were to be sold to the farmers in
Missouri and Kansas to raise money
to buy food. We got to find another
route back to New York though because
those farmers are threatening to thresh
us on sight if they see us again. The
only money anybody's seen is what the
Korean stealth air force dropped on us the day
you demonstrated the efficacy of the
Money Chant. I got to hand it to you
though. We picked up enough chump
change from those farmers to keep us in
Kimchi on the cob for the next seven
years. But I sure could go for a big
Mac Manna burger from heaven.

            MONEY
Patience my perfect potential mate. I
promise you (Pronounced filly
mig non) filet mignon for the spirit
when I make my dedication speech
from the top of the holy mountain tomorrow.
Then we will both rest and pray for a day
before going back to Scarsdale. Mountain

air is so erecting to the spirit. Come on
now. Let's get to that Grand Teton. On
your feet girl. Show that ole pioneer
spirit. Stop loafing. Your female soft-
ness is raining on my parade.

FANNY jumps up lightly but the REVEREND is not so lucky. He struggles to his feet only to collapse back on the ground.

FANNY
I'm ready FATHER.

MONEY.
SATAN has invaded my left foot. I must
exorcise my foot of this evil demon and
cast it into a herd of buffalo.

FANNY
But there is no herd of buffalo or pigs
or anything else FATHER.

MONEY
How about women? No good. They are already demons. I will cast it into this
Rastafarian voodoo hemp walking pipe
I won on a missionary cruise to Jamaica and
we will sell replicas as Devil's Pipe
Divining Rods. Now listen to this SATAN.
In the name of Ludwig Von Braun, Dee Pack
Chopper, and Shirley McVane, I command
you outta my foot or I'll cane you within
an inch of your life. (Hits left toe)
Ouch! I conjure you by the God of the
ancient Egyptians Isis, go hence thou who
comest in darkness, whose nose job is
turned backwards, whose face is two,
whose tongue has seven forks and two
spoons. Hast thou come to kiss
my clean toes with thy unclean sulfurous
breath? I conjure thee by him who mani-

fested himself to Osreal by night in a
pillar of fire and brought down on the
Pharaoh the ten plagues because he would
not hearken. I conjure thee demonic
spirit, out of my big toe and I promise
thee a new home in Dennis Rodmac who
knows a lot more about abomination than
I ever will. O.K. That did it for
sure. Get down and be my step up. Show
some respect for MONEY.

FANNY gets down on all fours allowing REV. MONEY to sit on her back as he attempts to get up. He finally collapses on top of her almost breaking her back.

                        FANNY
Oh I think my back is broken. Oh FATHER.
I think the super God over you has done
this trick to you that you may yet demon-
strate your divinity. If you can't go
to the mountain, why don't you perform a
miracle and have the mountain come to you?

                        MONEY
Yeah! Great idea number two. If you
keep coming up with ideas like this, I
may soon announce that I will forego the
usual seven year waiting period and allow
you to become the perfect REVEREND
MOTHER MRS. MONEY. Now then.
Watch this. I've never cared for those hip-
hopping Mohammedans because they got
the tattoo of Cain on them. I can out do any
rap job that Mohammed ever came up with.
Watch this. I'll not only make that mountain
come to me, but I'm going to make it
kiss my tush. (FANNY interjects. "Toe
FATHER. Watch the bloopers".)

"Mountain mountain mountain high.
This is the moon moon moon rapping.
Teton Teton Teton high you must come
and kiss my toe or die. And SATAN
can kiss my blooper ass. (The lights
and sound could be made to reflect
the displeasure of the mountain. A
deep rumbling recorded laugh maybe)
Hey you overgrown set of mammarys.
You mother of abomination.
You obscenity on the horizon.
You overgrown anthill.
This is the REV. MOON SUN MONEY
and I'm a son of a bulldozer when
I get mad. I have a red belt in
Tae Kwon Do and if you don't come
here and kiss my toe, I'll give
you a kick that'll land you in
Frozen North Chosen.
(the mountain begins to quiver with
fear. Ripple the flat or something else)
You see. It's working. It crapped
an avalanche. Teton Teton Teton high,
come and kiss my toe or I'll buy
you and donate you as a Hare Krishna
jumping jerk chanting center. The vibra-
tions from their chanting will turn
you into a shell-shocked shivering
shadow of your former majesty in a
week. Let me give you an example."
(REV. MONEY chants nam ryoho renge
kwo, the wrong chant but he gets
the right results. FANNY is so frightened
during the ensuing lightening storm
and blackout that she lets out a
loud kissing sound that MONEY thinks is
the mountain kissing his foot.
When the lights come up...)

MONEY
I did it. I did it. I really am
the Messiah. Did you hear the
mountain kiss my toe?

FANNY
Praise be to the Messiah REV.
MOON SUN MONEY. This was a real
certified grade A miracle from the
same folks who brought you the celestial yo yo, the devil's hemp divining
rod, Ginseng Scotch, the Money Chant,
and now Teton kisses straight from the
baloney stone. (BLACKOUT)

CURTAIN SCENE V/ CURTAIN SCENE VI

There is a speaker's platform decorated with patriotic trappings. Next to the platform is a statue covered by a cloth. FANNY makes her entrance alone greeting the gathered multitude of MONEYCHILDREN (Audience) as a warm up speaker for the REV. MONEY dedication speech. She teaches various devious ways to sell various devious Church of Money divinely deceptive products.

FANNY
Greetings MONEYCHILDREN. There
will be a slight delay while the make-up
men prepare the REV. MONEY to face the
television cameras, which will make this
speech a worldwide event. Have patience.
Television is as demanding of Messiahs
as it is of ordinary people. Let me
remind you that the duties of a MONEYCHILD
are both sacred and profane. The blessed
FATHER instructs you in sacred responsibilities and he has put me in charge of
the profane. Messiah's are not sent to
earth to deal with mundane matters like
money. The REVEREND must be available

at all times for consultations with God
who phones regularly on the divine line.
But all those calls are beginning to add
up and we must therefore think of making
money for MONEY. Never forget that all
money that doesn't belong to God belongs
to SATAN and any method used to take it
away from him is O.K. It is a cardinal
rule of this church that we must be more
devious than he is in order to triumph.
When we acquire SATAN'S money, his power
becomes ours too. The blessed FATHER is
creating a new Jerusalem in Korea. It
will be called MONEYLAND, the Disneyland
of North Korea. And if you want a place
in this heaven on earth, you'll have to
earn it. You can do this by selling our
new line of products, all blessed and
approved by the savior himself. First
and most perishable are peanuts. These
are specially treated to create an
immediate craving for our Gacseng Daniels
which will be a sellout at $5.00 a shot.
Then we have special floating platform
shoes for walking on water. What they
really do is teach humility to those who
aspire to miracles that can only be
performed by God or MONEY. Our personal
hygiene division has cornered the condom
bubble gum market and is now declaring
war on evil odors with Smote an all purpose douche, mouthwash and deodorant.
The entertainment division announces the
release of a new record album, the REV.
MONEY Sings, which will be an even bigger
smash than his first bullet the REVEREND
MONEY SPEAKS, because it is in English
and has a pogo beat. Yes children, the
Messiah is what is happening and I hope
we can supply you with enough REV. MONEY

Superstar Tornado Trooper jump suits to meet demand. And I am happy to announce that some of you nubile young virgins have been selected for special pilgrimages to Washington D.C. to make legal campaign contributions. You will be entrusted with fat little envelopes to be used if any additional persuasion is necessary. Always remember that anything is all right as long as you do it for MONEY. And don't forget to pick up your price lists and sample kits after the REVEREND'S speech. Now, he's ready. The divine leader who showed us the light. The FATHER who brought us out of the darkness. The last hope for a spiritual world based on pure greed. The REV.MOON SUN MONEY!

There is a roar from the crowd and a chant of "we want MONEY" and MONEY finally takes the microphone.

MONEY

Moneychildren, militia patriots, douche peddlers, con artists for God, lend me your bowels. We have come here not to praise REV MONEY port-a-johns but to dedicate a statue to the greatest mouthwash bag to sit in the oval office in history. On this solemn date 4 scores and seven blowjobs ago, freedom, in fact license, first reared its beautiful, solemn and sometimes-virgin maidenhead. And even more important, generosity burst forth from the bowels of anonymity with such force as to almost bankrupt the mother in childbirth. This is why we stand here before you, your humble savior, on the most suckled out breast in the world, the very teat that feeds and nourishes

everything that is still sacred. But this
great mammary is in deadly danger from
the forces of SATANIC hell. The forces
of SATAN are everywhere poised at the
slightest sign of weakness to pounce on
this chaste breast and tear forth with
treacherous poison fangs the tender heart
that beats within. That is why I come
to you to be your savior. I am ready to
do battle with the great SATAN to the last
drop of my money. Of course it is not going
to be easy to get it away from your parents.
Once in a millennium there appears a
prophet who like John the Baptist cried
in the wilderness to announce a new era
of blessedness. Such a prophet recently
appeared in this land, but like most
prophets, he got the bums rush by his own
own people. This saintly politician was
the most talented blacklister, scapegoater,
bugger and SATAN hunter of all
time. I hope you don't think I have an
anal fixation if I tell you he gave it
to SATAN right up the old Yin-Yang. He was
like most precocious penises way ahead
of his time. Think of the balls of it.
Hiring plumbers to plug leaks by buggering
government employees. And he buggered
himself the most. Auto-sodomaic recording
will one day be recognized as being as
American an institution as moms own apple
pie. Let's hear three cheers for the greatest
bugger in history. (No one cheers) Alas,
he is gone, the victim of some of SATAN'S
most sulfurous tricks, but not forgotten.
There before you hidden for the moment by
a piece of drapery is a solid chocolate
statue of this great champion of freedom.
Naturally we will be marketing facsimiles
of this statue to be sold on every street

corner in America. To maximize the value
of this heretic-hunting fetish, I am
canonizing him as the first saint of the
Church of Money. Remove the cover from
the blessed SAINT NIXON. (In place of
the NIXON'S statue is one of Smoky the Bear
with a green face. (The preceding can be changed
to a different person. Any ideas?)

FANNY
(Fanny reads) It says, "Dedicated to Smoky the
Bear, died from eating a dangerous statue."

MONEY
Who's the practical joker? My divine
eyes are offended by this blasphemous act.
SATAN has struck me in the back, but
I will strike back twice as hard. I
control this country through my campaign
contributions in Washington. My virgins
have been doing their work well. The
divine principal will soon be the law of
this lawless land. I won't stand for
graffiti, pranksterteering or comedians.
I shall ban Halloween. I've had it with
the four freedoms in this country. I
came here originally to take advantage of
them, but I have discovered that if you
give them four, they'll want five and on
and on until you have anarchy. To the
masses freedom means the license to commit
every unclean act. This is wrongheaded-
ness. Only God is free. That's all I have
to say. I'll let my deputy say whatever
profane things I feel in my heart.

FANNY
The Messiah must leave because he has
broken out in pimples of wrath and wants
to see the Divine's makeup man for a cure. He

also wants to announce that bear meat is
Manna from heaven and anyone who burns
down a national forest will be made a
Saint of the Church of Money.

CURTAIN SCENE VI/ CURTAIN/SCENE VII

In the darkness there is heard the oooing and ahing of lovemaking. When the lights come up the REV. and FANNY are at rest having just made love. She is wearing sexy Victoria's Secret lingerie and he old-fashioned boxer shorts or they could be in their Karate suits. Whatever will get the best laugh.

                FANNY
Money money money money. (Both laugh)
I've never been able to say that with
quite so much feeling.

                MONEY
Oh... that felt so good.

                FANNY
It was great. I can hardly believe you
never did that before.

                MONEY
Well it's true. It's the first time I've
ever had horizontal Tae Kwon Do.

                FANNY
Um... You're either a quick study or I'm
a good teacher.

                MONEY
I think it's a combination of both. I
don't care. You were great.

                FANNY
Helps to be divinely inspired.

MONEY
I wasn't trying so hard the first time.

FANNY
Wow. I'm impressed. That was some workout.

MONEY
(Laughs crazily) Is it like this all the time?

FANNY
Sometimes it's better.

MONEY
Really! Oh I'm glad, I'm really glad we finally got it together. I'm glad I didn't do it with anybody else.

FANNY
Was I worth waiting for?

MONEY
You were worth waiting for, believe me.

FANNY
So were you.

MONEY
Did you seduce me? Was I an easy lay?

FANNY
No, it wouldn't be an easy thing to seduce you.

MONEY
You can be sure of one thing, you got it made now.

FANNY
What's my fortune cookie? Half your fortune? Um...

MONEY
Sure, we'll get married and I'll inform the organization that you are the perfect blessed REV. MOTHER MRS. MONEY. You'll stand next to me at all the public functions. You'll speak at luncheons. You'll have your own private airplane... just like the wife of the President of the United States.

FANNY
Will I get paid?

MONEY
You'll be on the payroll.

FANNY
Sounds very tempting, almost devilishly tempting.

MONEY
Sure... It's yours. You've got it.

FANNY
Oh I don't know... I've always been used to earning my own living.

MONEY
Sure... You'll be working for the cause, promoting, organizing, teaching, selling subverting, spying, lying, unifying, lobbying, bribing, and maybe even seducing sometimes... You learn so quickly. I'm lucky to have you. When do you want to set the date?

FANNY
I don't think I'm ready for marriage
though. I'm not. No, I don't want to
get married yet.

MONEY
O.K. We'll just live together for awhile.

FANNY
But what'll you tell your followers about
pre-marital celibacy?

MONEY
They won't know anything. I'll just tell
them I've decided not to spawn a master
race for a while. It'll all be done by artifi-
cial insemination from a sperm bank I am
creating. You and I will be doing it on
the side and nobody will know the difference. It'll just be REV. MONEY AND
FANNY MARTIN and I'll make you the
successor. You'll be the heir to the throne.
How do you like that?

FANNY
I don't know. That throne. I think I'd
have to re-do that throne room a bit to
suit me.

MONEY
What do you want to do? Redecorate
that throne room?

FANNY
Yes. I think it needs it.

MONEY
Yes, I think it needs it too. Go ahead
and re-decorate.

FANNY
I really wish I could marry you. I've been giving it a lot of thought, but now that I've had you, I think there may be greater heights to scale. I think I want to go back to being a nymphomaniac psychologist.

MONEY
Wait a minute. What did you say?

FANNY
I said I want to go back to being a nymphomaniac psychologist.

MONEY
Am I hearing right?

FANNY
You heard it twice.

MONEY
I'll understan... Where did this come from? How did you get this idea into your head?

FANNY
Well, I enjoy helping mankind in my own way.

MONEY
You can help them best through the organization. I mean you can help defeat SATAN and convert everybody to MONEYANITY. Look dear; this is going to be a partnership. Think of the bucks we'll rake in off of all the gimmicks we've got.

FANNY
That sounds fine, but I have to leave.

MONEY
Well, why do you have to go back to what
you were doing before? Why can't you
stay with me?

FANNY
I need a challenge and I've had you and
my challenge is gone.

MONEY
What'll you mean, you've had me and your
challenge is gone. What kind of thing
is that to say?

FANNY
When you've had one Korean, you've had
them all.

MONEY
(Screaming in rage) What'll what'll,
where is this coming from? You've been
trying to get me since you joined this
church and now that you've got me, now
you tell me I'm just like anybody else.
That's blasphemous.

FANNY
It's just like oriental food. When you've
had one meal, you need another one an
hour later.

MONEY
I've never heard of anything like this
in my life. You want to leave the organization? Go away? And I'll bet anything
your parents do not even want you back.

FANNY
Yep... I'm going to start my own organization.

MONEY
Oh... I didn't hear that, oooooooh...

FANNY
Nymphomaniacs anonymous. And to finance
that, I shall put these experiences here
to beneficial use by incorporating them
into a book. A book that will detail
intimately my experiences and exposing
you for the unholy trinity of a fraud
that you are.

MONEY
You're going to write an expose?

FANNY
Yes. I think it's time people wised up
to you. You say you are trying to save
the world from SATAN? How come your
whole organization is composed of
communes filled with your slavish followers?
And you sit there dictating their entire
lives. Sounds pretty SATANIC to me.

MONEY
My dear, you're confusing subtle free
enterprise with communism. There's a
very important difference. I'm in charge.

FANNY
A slave by any other name would be the
same.

MONEY
How can you do this to me? You've got
half the whole gold mine locked up.

FANNY
It's not enough. I need to know that
I have the power to destroy it totally
and you with it.

MONEY
What do you want to destroy it for? So
it's a little communist. So what? So
are corporations and no one cares that they
are raping and pillaging the world. We're
a little Fascist too. What's wrong with
wanting to destroy your enemies? But
most of all, we also believe in democracy,
which is the dictatorship of the majority.
All of these things are good if they are
unified. That is what we are trying to do.
Unify all things. Why do you want to destroy me? I am the divine knot that holds
everything together.

FANNY
You're full of Kimchi. I don't want some
ignorant Korean who doesn't even speak
English to come into this country trying
to take over. And trying to make American
women submissive. I don't like that. I
don't like you. You might be good in bed,
but man you got a lot of other things
Those just don't jive.

MONEY
Sweetheart, if it jives in bed, nothing
else matters.

FANNY
Well, if we can meet on the side once
in a while, but my course is set. It's
time for the world to know that a woman is
God.

MONEY
Ridiculous.

FANNY
The era of the schlong is gone.

MONEY
The era of the schlong is gone?

FANNY
Yes. The era of the schlong is gone.
This is the era of the clit.

MONEY
No no no no no no...

FANNY
This is the era of the clit. You're worn
out. You're dried up. You've had it.
A super brain has had you.

MONEY
No honey. You're just a cheap lay.

FANNY
I didn't know you'd had enough experience
to judge.

MONEY
Well there's a lot about me that you don't
know sweet tits. Do you think you've
fucked me? Bull schlong! I've been in-
seminating you since you walked into my
throne room at the Waldorf. I've been
playing the fool, but now in the final
revelation you see that REV. MONEY
really knows where it's at. And it'll
never be the year of the clit. It'll continue to
be the year of the schlong onward and
onward forever. And you see that mob

out there? They're going to continue to get fucked until they wise up. (Sticks out tongue at crowd.)

                    FANNY
Well SATAN, I've wised up. I'm leaving, but I'll be sure to think of you when I'm on my FANNY MARTIN throne taking my morning constitutional, if you haven't been crucified by the time I get back to N.Y.C. (She exits laughing)

                    MONEY
She's joking. She's got to be joking. This is some kind of strange American sense of humor unknown in Korea. Come back FANNY. I'll give you the whole goldmine. I love you.

                    FANNY
(Off stage) See you in hell SATAN honey.

                    MONEY
A plague on her and her house. I don't need her. And I don't care what she says about me, because my kind are in control of the media. What does bother me is that crack she made about me being SATAN. How can I be SATAN when God is chairman of the board? Watch this! (Calls from a red phone) This is REV. MOON SUN MONEY calling. Would you put me through to God? Which one? What a dumb question. Everybody knows monopoly is the 99th commandment... What, he has many facets like a woman? Well let me speak to the unified facet. Hello FATHER, I'm having big trouble with a woman. You are too? Why don't you smite her? She's your better half?

How strange. Can you smote mine for me...
Women are a necessary evil? But I'd rather
be celibate... I'm an incompetent asswhole?
Yes FATHER I do have one more request.
Can I be a savior without being a martyr?
I don't want to be a martyr, because martyrs
are crucified and that's an anachronistic idea...
Can't let me out alive? But... Sure I want
to be famous... Can't be a superstar without
violence? How about if I become a porno
star? You prefer violence to sex? But
I just had the most interesting experience.
Sex is wonderful... It causes overpopulation? We were cuter when we were
monkeys? Don't you want a master race?
He hung up! (Back to audience) You see.
Everything is fine. I have to admit I've had a
couple of setbacks, but I haven't built
my house on sand. The foundation of my
divine principal is laid in pure plutonium.
I've built my house like a nuclear bomb
just to prove I stand for everything
righteous anyone ever thought of. And
that is why I will get bigger and bigger
until I control the buttons that release
the energy of the sun on earth. Then we
will have the power to exorcise evil once
and for all. Me SATAN? No way my friends.
I am not a tempter. I offer you nothing
but a trade. You hand over your worldly
goods and I will give you eternal life.
As you are leaving the theater, just leave
a blank check with your signature on it,
made out to me the Church of Money. It is
your ticket to Moneyland, the Kingdom of
Heaven on earth. Thank you for listening
and may you value your lives enough to
become converts to Moneyanity.

FINI

* Copyright infringement disclaimer.

This play was written in the mid 1970's. It was cast and put in rehearsal at about the same time. Parts of the play were improvised by the actors, some of which was subsequently incorporated into the script. The ownership of such actor additions becomes the property of the play, as far as I understand the law regarding this. I did not have a public performance of this play until about ten years later when it was presented at the Hollywood Hilltop Theater in Los Angeles starring Bonnie Bradigan as Fanny Martin and myself as Reverend Money. In the interim years, one skit in the play was stolen and used almost word for word in a television series episode. I do not know the circumstances of how this theft came about. As the play was not copyrighted at the time, I did not sue or check into the circumstances. I have not changed that part of my script from the original written in the 1970's. It is presented here just the way it was collaborated and recorded and subsequently presented. This disclaimer is not intended to harm the reputation of any honest person, as the circumstances by which this came about may have been perfectly innocent except by the actions of the currently unknown perpetrator. I will not, however, bastardize my play to exculpate the guilty party or protect myself from counter claims. This is the only play published in this book that was written with the help of improvisation. It was first however written as a complete script and the ad-libs or improves that were added later became part of the play by the authors choice.   Ed Wode

THE DEMAGOGUES

A four-act play

Written

By

Ed Wode

Copyright © 2006
By Ed Wode
edwode@gmail.com

THE DEMAGOGUES
A four-act play

CAST OF CHARACTERS

DIANA, THE HUNTRESS
BARRY MAD CAL PANASSES
GENERAL ULYSSIUS S. AGAMEMNON
HERCULES AGNEW
ORACALLIS
MARCHELLO MACHIAVELLI
APHRODISI
ARCHON JASON
LADY LYSISTRATA JASON, SR.
LYSISTRATA JASON, JR.
GENERAL MALISIUSES GEORGISIUS
KING KRUSHAMEMNON
QUEEN KRUSHAMEMNON
PRINCE ATLAS KRUSHAMEMNON
SOCRATES
ARISTOPHENES
DIODOTUS
STOOLITES
TRAGIC ACTOR
CURITHIAS
O'HARA
ZEUS

THE DEMAGOGUES

ACT I, SCENE I

A public bath in ancient Athens, 5th century B.C. At the rise, a TV reporter for the E-ZEUS heavenly TV network is speaking to the ubiquitous Eye of ZEUS TV camera. This is a stealth crew and cannot be seen by mortals such as the ones now in the bath.

                DIANA THE HUNTRESS
Gods and goddesses of the civilized universe. This is DIANA the
HUNTRESS once again coming to you
for the E-ZEUS heavenly TV network
that brings you the amusing and entertaining war of the week. This
week we are going to focus on gossip
as there is a boring temporary lull
in the fighting. I know you all
love a choice tidbit of gossip almost
as much as you love war. Listen up.
There is going to be a peace conference
held soon that if successful could be a
ratings disaster for this network.
This is a dangerous precedent that
must be stopped at all costs or
we Gods may be doomed to eternal
boredom. After a mere seven years
of warfare, the ever folly prone,
but highly entertaining ATHENIANS
have agreed to talk peace with their
mortal enemies the laconic Spartan
bores. And this worst of all possible
follies is in spite of the fact that they
have won their first great victory at sea
and trapped a mighty SPARTAN led
army on the little island of SPHAGIAE.
The latest scuttlebutt has it that the brave

infanticidally prone SPARTANS who
have always had the advantage in the
war prior to this setback are willing
to make peace with the ATHENIANS on
humiliatingly honorable terms. The
only hope for continued carnage is
that the ATHENIANS, inflamed by their
pyrrhic victory, will make such in-
sultingly stringent terms that the
proud but dumb SPARTANS will turn
them down. Both states are hampered
in their negotiations by glorious
factions that wish to continue the
war until the other side is annihilated.
Just such a group of lovable rascals is
the little group of marvelously mean
spirited little men you see here before you.
 Let us stealthily listen in. I will assume
the role of a serving boy and serve wine.

The four men in the bath (Alternately in a wine shop at the AGORA) have been having an animated conversation about the peace proposal. They are all hawks on continuing the war with SPARTA for their own selfish reasons. BARRY MAD CAL PANASSESS, the orator, because he has been hired by the hawks to advocate their position: GENERAL ULYSSIUS. S. AGAMEMNON, because he wants glory and loot; HERCULES AGNEW, because he profits on war by selling arms; and ORACALLIS, the oracle, because people consult him about the vicissitudes of war. BARRY MAD CAL is getting a massage. The general is drunk and getting drunker. ORACALLIS, who is a touch swishy, pinches "the boy wine server" now and then. DIANA gets pissed and slaps him.

 ORACALLIS
Ouch! This boy has a wallop like
a 600 lb gorilla god.

 GENERAL
If you can tell the future as you
claim oracle, you should have known

better.

ORACALLIS
I can very accurately tell the future my dear GENERAL ULYSSIUS S. AGAMEMNON, but I can't account for the dirty tricks of the frivolous frog friggin Gods. I am only a mortal man and subject to their farting in the face of fate just as you are. I am like a blind beggar who must trust his every step to the capriciousness of their malignity. Except for their cupidity, I'd be the richest man in ATHENS.

GENERAL
You promised me victory over the SPARTANS and by the gods you were right.

DIANA
(Aside) Lucky for the lout there was a great fog and the Spartans attacked each other. Even so the ATHENIANS suffered severe losses of ships and men.

ORACALLIS
But you lost many ships. The mob thinks you reckless with their lives.

GENERAL
I was put on this earth to harvest human life the way a farmer has been put here to make fine wine out of the vine. He knows that by crushing the fruit the future will bring him a vintage year. War is the

wine of the gods.

> ORACALLIS
> Are you not some god in disguise
> that you are so callous toward
> human suffering?

> GENERAL
> Sheep are fit for the skewer. Why
> not people? (Taking a deep gulp
> of wine) Why not see the world from
> a soldier's vantage point?

> ORACALLIS
> Thru the bottom of a bottle of
> bad wine.

> GENERAL
> You cowardly tea bag. Why don't you
> join my navy and I'll demonstrate
> to you how I win the victories I
> pay you to predict?

> ORACALLIS
> And help you conquer the anchovies?

> GENERAL
> Is cowardliness so unmanning that
> even a talent for favorable prophesy
> cannot bolden this dress wearing
> capon? I would sooner have women in
> my navy.

DIANA is furious at this aspersion to femininity and almost skewers the general.

> ORACALLIS
> If I am a coward, at least I'm not
> stupid enough to let the ATHENIANS
> appoint me a general after all of
> my predecessors have been put to

death for their failures. Only
a social climbing common dunce
would be such a fool.

> GENERAL

Stupid. Common am I? Because the
nobility are all cowards like you?
Your runaway slave HERODIOUS boxed
your ears before he ran off to
SPARTA. He chased you out of the
the house whipping you like a dog
until you begged for mercy. And
soon, he will be back to put you
and your precious nobility out of
your city unless I am allowed to
destroy him and all the SPARTANS
once and for all.

> BARRY

And why has it taken you seven years
to achieve your first victory?

> GENERAL

My predecessors were besotted bumb-
ling sentimental effete nobility more
concerned with winning Olympic
sports than slaughtering youth for
the glory of ATHENS. That's why.
I have only had the supreme command
for two years and already I am in a
position to destroy the SPARTAN
host. And now the politicians want
to make peace. Give me another
drink boy!

> BARRY

He's right ORACALLIS. Their army
is trapped on the small island of
SPHAGIAE. Now is our chance to
utterly scourge them from the face

of the earth. Then we can unite
all GREECE under ATHENIAN democracy.

    ORACALLIS
Bah, humbug. We have heard it all
before my dear BARRY. I do not trust
the puffery of generals who are always hungry for glory and greedy for
loot; at the expense of other men's
lives I might add.

    BARRY
Are you for peace then?

    ORACALLIS
I am for peace, ZEUS be my witness, if every last SPARTAN is dead
or a slave. They can never be
trusted to keep the peace. At the
first opportunity they will attempt to
destroy us and everything we stand
for.

    BARRY
Then you are for war. But can we
win? I too am for war. But only
the kind that are won.

    ORACALLIS
The majority of the gods, ZEUS help
them, are on our side. They hate
SPARTAN gravity just a little more
than they are jealous of the ATHEN-
IAN ability to deceive the world by
bragging they have invented everything
including the wheel. They cry out in
one thunderous voice for the annihilation
of those unnatural SPARTANS who
forsake the natural pleasures of life
in favor of hardship and deprivation.

But harken to this! How can one ever
be certain of victory in war? The
gods, like men, can always be bribed.
A liberal sprinkle of gold on their
altars and they would sell their
mothers for fish bait.

          GENERAL
When ATHENS opens its tight fist
and gives me enough money to buy
the arms I need, you shall have your
victory. With enough money I will
skewer the whole world.

          HERCULES
GENERAL ULYSSIUS S. AGAMEMNON
is right soothsayer. Gold makes war
run as smoothly as it does other things.

          BARRY
Then donate some gold to my election campaign HERCULES AGNEW. If
you wish to continue this war, you
must grease some palms. Help me get
elected ARCHON of ATHENS and I will
empty the treasury buying swords
and spears from you.

          HERCULES
(Gives Oracallis a coin) What are his chances
of winning soothsayer?

          ORACALLIS
It is written in the stars that in this year
of our gods, 1000 A.G.*, that BARRY
MAD CAL PANASSES, JR. is going to
be elected ARCHON of ATHENS unless
there is campaign finance reform.

*DIANA interjects "after goatskins" after "A.G".

> BARRY
> Is this true or are you just saying
> this because I bought you a new
> crystal ball?

> ORACALLIS
> Was not your ass breeder father Barry Mad
> Cow Panasses, Sr. declared by the assem-
> bly to be the infallible God of asses when
> he departed? Are not you a chip off the ole
> block?

> BARRY
> I don't know which fork of your
> tongue I prefer. The insulting
> or the fawning.

> GENERAL
> (Now very drunk) He forks with his ass
> and lies with his tongue. Why not çut it
> out and teach him to lie with his hands.

ORACALLIS flips him the bird. The drunken GENERAL half in jest and half for real staggers after him trying to cut him to pieces. ORACALLIS undaunted, expressing himself in universal sign language, uses every curse word in the GREEK tongue to taunt the general. The others laugh.

> BARRY
> You are better off leaving him with
> his tongue. He makes lies to you far
> worse with his hands. He just called
> you a mother of Satyrs and a chicken
> buggier.

> GENERAL
> (Really mad) There'll be nothing
> left of him but a butt for jokes

by the time I am through with him.

                    BARRY
A butt for jokes? That's a new idea.
Methinks you are drunk dear general.
Let the wretch go. Here is a gold
drachma ORACALLIS. I wish to know
the minds of the gods. Are they for
war or peace soothsayer?

                    ORACALLIS
The vast majority favor war, but
OLYMPUS is not a democracy. It all
depends on which side the judges
decide to bet on.

                    BARRY
That's no answer. I want my money
back.

                    GENERAL
You see. He mocks us. Let me geld
him and he will be as pliable as two
women, since he is already one.

DIANA has had enough. She hits the general over the head with a bottle and he falls to the floor out cold.

                    BARRY
            I demand a refund.

                    ORACALLIS
No refunds, but a little more gold
and I think I can afford enough of
a bribe to get you a straight answer.

BARRY gives him another gold drachma. ORACALLIS closes his eyes and concentrates.

ORACALLIS
The most powerful gods have wagered
heavily that the war will continue.

BARRY
Just as I thought. And if we make
peace, we lose favor with the gods.
I must win this election. Our present Archon JASON is a peace loving
fool.

HERCULES
Wise words BARRY MAD CAL. Your
words can make men of the cowardly rabble,
but only gold can make them
ravening beasts. Here is a campaign
contribution. (He gives him a bag
of gold.)

BARRY
(Savoring the bag of gold) I thank
the gods for favoring an enterprise
so profitable. The mob will soon
hear this good news. And we shall
have war, war, war.

ORACALLIS
(Aside) I must quickly to the SPARTANS
and sell them the same good news.
I cannot lose.

DIANA
(Aside drunk) And I must be off to the
island of LESBOS and celebrate
this victory with my sisters.

HERCULES
(Aside) And I must be off to the
AGORA and see if I can corner the

market on caskets.

GENERAL
(Recovering consciousness, but drunk)
It will be a sacrilege to stay alive.
The geeks and nerd draft dodgers will
inherit the earth. Ops! I better watch my
mouth. Our leaders are the worst draft
dodgers of all.

BARRY
Come all you cowards, pederasts,
drunks, fools and loafers; I am
your fearless leader. I promise
you full employment. War always
brings prosperity. (Aside) At least
for orators.

HERCULES
Bring me your plows that I may turn
them into swords. I can't lose. I
turn them back into plows when the
war ends. The best formula for turning a profit is to churn war and peace.
I am just like a farmer except that
instead of growing potatoes I grow
severed limbs. They make finger licking
delicious dog food too.

BARRY
The mob rules. Long live the mob.

THE MOB
(In the distance) Long live BARRY.
ARCHON of ATHENS.

ORACALLIS
(Aside) BARRY is a great demagogue
who knows how to fool the mob by
telling them everything they want

to hear but the truth. There is
nothing deader than yesterday's
news except a politician who tells
the truth.

           THE MOB
Long live BARRY, etc.

           ORACALLIS
I just received an important message.
from the heavens. According to DIANA, the
Huntress, ZEUS' lesbo spokesperson he has
granted hereditary godhood to the PANASSESS
family, or was it the talking donkey MR.
OEDIPUS? Whatever. It's not
important. Apotheosis by any name is the same.
BARRY has been elevated to godhood. Hail to
BARRY! Hail to MAD CAL PANASSES, God
of asses.

All cheer BARRY and hail him as a god.

CURTAIN
ACT I, SCENE I

CURTAIN
ACT I, SCENE II

This scene takes place in the TEMPLE OF APOLLO near Pylos, Greece. JASON, his wife HELEN and daughter LYSISTRATA are coming to pay their respects to APOLLO. The high priestess APHRODISI has been entertaining MARCHELLO MACHIAVELLI the ROMAN ambassador and spy. He has seduced APHRODISI so that he can spy on the Greeks and learn their deepest secrets. He sneaks up on her from behind and surprises her. She is not happy to see him, as she would be executed if it were known that they were having an affair

MARCHELLO
Guess who?

APHRODISI
Who? You mad Roman slave! Are you
still lurking about? You must leave
and by the back door. Quickly! It
would not do for a Roman spy to be
found seeking advice or other favors
in a Greek temple. Our people are
very jealous of their gods.

MARCHELLO
You mean if they find out you are
not a virgin, you'll be boiled in
oil?

APHRODISI
It's you I am thinking of. They
would do unspeakable things to you.
I would have to call you sister.

MARCHELLO
I am not frightened. I must hear what
position JASON will take in the peace
conference. Rome must know.

APHRODISI
You dare ask treason of the high
priestess of APOLLO?

MARCHELLO
What are you worried about? APOLLO
has a large bet on the SPARTANS to
win this war according to ORACALLIS
the soothsayer. Don't you want to
help your boss?

APHRODISI
You dare to mention that double deal-

ing crystal ball fondling faker to me?

MARCHELLO
It is in your interest as much as mine to prevent peace. Yours because you've taken bribes from both sides for APOLLO'S favor and mine because I share my countries ambition to conquer Greek temple priestesses.

APHRODISI
I must be mad as Mad Cal letting you pull that cheap Roman trick on me. Coming in here dressed as APOLLO himself. I truly thought you were the god until you proved less than a god in bed.

MARCHELLO
You did it for religion and I did it for Rome. If only everything done for God and country had such a happy ending.

A trumpet announces the arrival of JASON and family.

APHRODISI
JASON is here. Quickly! Out the back window.

MARCHELLO
Not until you tell me you love me and will help me trick JASON into continuing the war against Sparta.

APHRODISI
I love you, but I will only help you because it is to APOLLO'S

benefit.

MARCHELLO
APOLLO will soon be the richest god
in Greece my dear. (Aside) And a
Roman convert.

MARCHELLO exists just as JASON and his entourage sweep in bearing bribes for APOLLO'S favor; euphemistically called gifts.

APHRODISI
Welcome to the temple of APOLLO,
JASON o great leader of the Athenian
people. The god is much pleased
by your visit.

JASON
We are much pleased to be here.
This is my wife Lysistrata and my
daughter Lysistrata.

APHRODISI
I can see they are worthy of so
great a leader of the Athenians.
It has been rumored they are
too godlike to be mere mortals.
Are they not goddesses in disguise?

JASON
Not likely. I'm proud to say they
are as modest as they are beautiful.

LADY JASON
I'm proud to say my neck is the only
part of me worthy of godhood. It is
way too good for this cheap bangle
given to me by the Roman ambassador.
He seduced me by pretending to be
APOLLO, son of a stallion. As it turned out, he was hardly more than a man.

I give this trinket to Apollo in the
hope that my husband JASON can forgive me for my natural mistake.

JASON
It is understandable. She has been
seduced by every other god and some
goddesses on Olympus.

LYSISTRATA
But mom! My neck is worthy of the
necklace. It is many degrees less
beautiful than yours. Just because
daddy is jealous of that Roman romantic who views himself as a Roman
stallion is no reason to insult
APOLLO with such a poor gift. Besides, daddy says he is going to
geld him and put him in a boy's
choir the next time he shows his
face.

MACHIAVELLI hiding behind the throne is not too happy to hear this and crosses himself. (A cheap anachronistic sight gag)

APHRODISI
An excellent fate for cheap Roman
romantics. This contemptible piece
of junk is much too poor for nobles
or goddesses, but is just right for
the neck of a dedicated virgin temple
priestess such as myself. You poor
wronged lady. Who beside myself
could resist such Roman villainy?

LYSISTRATA
(Aside in stage whisper) She doth protest
too well. (To priestess) I too am a virgin
great priestess. Can I too become a priestess
and take bribes for Apollo's favor?

JASON
Gifts for his pleasure LYSISTRATA.
Bribes are for politicians.

LADY JASON
What a good idea dear. Then you would get
to wear this necklace all the time.

JASON
(Aside) I would give the loot of Troy
to rid us of her ingenuous frankness.

LADY JASON
My daughter's fondest wish is to serve
APOLLO by remaining a virgin like your-
self-great and beautiful high priestess.

LYSISTRATA
I have heard that after APOLLO blesses
his priestesses there are many virgin births.

APHRODISI
I see you are just what we need here.
A chip off the old block. A politicians daughter as beautiful as a
babbling brook. Unfortunately there
is a very long waiting list at the
moment my dear. It is unbelievable
how many young women of HELLAS are
dying to dedicate themselves to virginity.

LYSISTRATA
(Sarcastic) How many? About two?

JASON
(Takes off gold chains) How long
did you say that list is?

LADY JASON
Yes. (Removes rings and other jewelry)
Perhaps these other bangles will shorten
the list to... (To JASON) what is
less than one my husband.

JASON
I don't know. We haven't invented
such a number yet, but I will put
my mathematicians to work on the
problem immediately.

APHRODISI
(Picking up the jewels) Perhaps there can
be an opening in a few weeks or months...
after you have destroyed the SPARTANS
and APOLLO has received half the plunder
from their cities.

LYSISTRATA
I have changed my mind. I have decided I will marry a SPARTAN after
we make peace with them.

APHRODISI is exasperated. JASON and LADY JASON start to take back their valuables.

LADY JASON
May I change the subject great priestess? I have a question of some
importance myself.

APHRODISI
Yes. If you stop being an Indian
giver and leave APOLLO something
worthy of his generosity in making
an appearance in the heavens each
day.

LADY JASON
(Dropping something) Of course. If
I could just know what is going
to be the fashion next season.

APHRODISI
Little will change, but that little
will make a great difference. You
know how men are.

LADY JASON
(Winks) My husband JASON is above
such lusting. (Drops another bangle)
But if you could be a little more
specific.

APHRODISI
Of course. Togas are going to be an inch
shorter and the left breast is going
to be exposed instead of the right.

LADY JASON
Marvelous! I'll have a matched set of
magnificent tan tits, marmalade flavor,
just as you like dear.

JASON
My dear! I'm shocked. Your alliteration
is borderline obscene my dove. You should
have said, I'll have a matched set of
mammary in 35 flavors just as Zeus likes.

LYSISTRATA
Humongous. Just the way you like them
Daddy.

LADY JASON
If you want to keep getting elected,
the most important thing to the easily
deceived mob is a well-dressed first
family.

APHRODISI
Right. Who cares about the flavor of
marmalade anyway? Beauty is what is
important.

LYSISTRATA
Could this be why I have so many
suitors since daddy became Archon?
All nerdy philosophers. All they do
is talk. I prefer the silent manly
SPARTAN youth. I think, after all,
you don't marry a man to talk to him.

LADY JASON
(Highly embarrassed) Lysistrata! Young
ladies of breeding do not think at all let alone
out of the box. Curb your tongue.

JASON
(Equally shocked) And if they do,
it is not to talk about their desire
for a suitor of an inferior race unless
he is filthy rich.

LYSISTRATA
I am only repeating common gossip
I heard in the market.

APHORDISI
One should never listen to opinions
of the common herd. They are an
ignorant and changeable mob who are
easily persuaded to believe the lies
and distortions of demagogues like
MAD CAL PANASSES, JR.

JASON
I resent that. My wife has some
blueblood, but I am a man of the

people.

APHRODISE
You are not as common as you think
JASON. You remember your grandfather
JASON the pirate? He confessed, just
before he was hung by the SPARTANS,
that he was the illegitimate son of
an Athenian nobleman.

LADY JASON
(Ecstatic) Oh JASON. You're one of
us.

JASON
Most beautiful and wise of high
priestesses, we must take leave of
you before our heads are turned so
far we take leave of our senses.

APHRODISI
Wait! Apollo has a question.

JASON
What can a humble man of the people
or should I say arrogant born again
nobleman be able to instruct a god
about?

APHRODISI
He wishes to know whether you will,
like a humble beggar, abjectly sue for
peace or arrogantly and nobly, as he
recommends, require stringent punitive
damages of the SPARTANS?

JASON
The latter I think. I will demand
of KING KRUSHIMEMNON of Sparta
great personal damages. One son, the

gods help him, to be married to my
daughter LYSISTRATA.

LYSISTRATA
(Jumping with joy) Father! You should
become an oracle. You speak in riddles
that befit the suitor.

APHRODISI
He makes vice a versa and versa nice.

JASON
Come ladies. It is getting late.

APHRODISI
May APOLLO always light your way
mighty JASON.

JASON
And may the light of peace shine
on you and the Greeks APHRODISI,
#1 virgin of the world.

Exeunt JASON and his family. Enter MARCHELLO furious.

MARCHELLO
What a spectacle. The Athenian takes
his god for a fool.

APHRODISI
Are you still here mad fiend from the
world below? My lust makes me a
fool. At least I have what should be
mine. This necklace is my rightful
bribe. You must have eaten an army of
your children before you broke down and
gave this bangle as a bribe.

MARCHELLO
Bribes are on the expense account, thank
the gods. Maybe I should take this peace
offering back. There will be peace.

APHRODISI
I did the best I could to seduce JASON
to a victory blessed by the gods.

MARCHELLO
Wait until the SPARTANS hear. You
also accepted their bribe for the
gods blessing on their enterprise.
If peace breaks out, you may be the
big loser. Our goose is cooked unless one of the war parties contrives
to sabotage the peace conference.
Our last best hope is MAD CAL
PANASSES, JR.

APHRODISI
The gods save us from that fool.
Have you no principles?

MACHIAVELLI
The first principle of being a diplomat is to have no principles my
dear virgin. A diplomat is like a
two legged bloodhound put on the
scent of his country's interests.
And I shall follow the scent of
MAD CAL until it leads to the doom
of Greece even if he does stink
higher than heaven. Speaking of
smells, I like that perfume you
are wearing. It is time for my Greek
lesson. And I don't mean vice versa.
Next to serving Rome, I love serving
Apollo.

APHORDISI
I will serve him too, but only under
protest. It is my sacred duty to
make converts.

END ACT I, SCENE II CURTAIN

CURTAIN UP ACT I, SCENE III

The Spartan home of KING KRUSHAMEMNON of Sparta. Chief of Staff of the Spartan army, GENERAL GEORGISIUS and the king have just finished wrestling. Slaves are rubbing them down.

GEORGI.
Some day I'll wring your royal neck.

KRUSH.
You have been trying for years.

GEORGI
This time the Athenians are doing
it for me.

KRUSH.
Why do you hate the idea of peace
so much? We are all Greeks.
And the Athenians have made some
great contributions to our civilization. Can you deny this?

GEORGI
Bah, humbug! Are a bunch of marble
statues of naked gods so much?

KRUSH
Their veneration of the contemplative
life has attracted some of our finest
youth.

GEORGI
A waste of masculinity.

KRUSH
I agree it is wasted on the poor,
but it gives a man of nobility
certain advantages. Even some generals have benefited by it.

GEORGI
That's a matter open for debate. If
you call rebelliousness, insubordination, riot, disorder, defiance,
unauthorized gaiety, devotion to
hedonism, and endless conversation
to be education, you can keep it.
But if you call the science of war,
sports, discipline, obedience of
orders, loyalty, devotion to duty,
manly arrogance, hatred of foreigners, and other Spartan beliefs
education, I am all for it.

KRUSH
You deny you can learn something
from an intelligent conversation?

GEORGI
This endless talk of the Athenians
leads to many dangerous ideas.
There is even one fool who claims
the world is round like a ball.

KRUSH.
I admit some of their ideas are preposterous, but equally harmless.
They have impressed the whole world
with the novelty of their ideas.

GEORGI
Harmless? Not so harmless. I fell
into a ditch on my face trying to

find out where this reputed circle
begins. And they demand slaves and
taxes for such harebrained ideas.

KRUSH.

We alone cannot withstand the great
king from Persia. And even in the
barbaric west there are some rude
crude and loud mouthed upstart road
masons encroaching on our territory.
We need strong allies like the Athenians used to be or some pip squeak
like Rome will one day be knocking
at our walls seeking our gold.

GEORGI

You sound like one of their notorious
demagogue orators, who for enough gold,
will take any issue, popular or unpopular,
just or unjust, mostly the latter and by all
manner of half truths, appeals to the emotions, and outright lies convince the dumb
uninformed mob of the rightness of
that bad cause. Soon you will be saying,
as they do, that they are the sole saviors of
Greece. Did not our 200 brave warriors
sacrifice themselves to keep the Persians
out? Are they not the greatest liars in
the history of the world?

KRUSH.

Yes. I agree. And their big talk
bragging has convinced the whole
world of the justice of their cause.
They, by the manner you just descri-
bed gain the support of the common
herd that fancies itself as having
a say in governing itself. All the
while the rich merchants pull the
strings behind the scenes and do as

they please cheating and pillaging
to their hearts content.

GEORGI
And their military might is opening
the whole world to this pillage. We
will not have to wait for the Persians to consume us. Unless we press
the attack and destroy them, we shall
be skewered and roasted like lamb
chops long before any barbarian has a
chance.

KRUSH.
Your argument is strong, but I am in
favor of making peace, at least until
we are strong enough to be assured of
victory. If we can make peace on
honorable terms, this will benefit
all HELLAS. If the Greeks could only
unite as one nation, we could bring
the benefits of our civilization to
the whole world.

GEORGI
To what end? The world is full of
savages who could never learn our
arts and sciences. And peace is the
way of cowards. It is best to make
war until the Athenian tyranny is
destroyed and Sparta is supreme.

KRUSH.
War is a risky game of chance. The
life of a nation depends on a roll
of the dice, the outcome of which
is never certain. Especially when
the gamble is against a bunch of
hard core gamblers like the Athenians.

GEORGI
Bah, humbug. They are not soldiers.
If we cannot defeat a lot of plague
faced philosophers and womanish
youth, we should fall on our swords
and colonize hell.

KRUSH.
These womanish youth have fought
us to a standstill for seven long
years. If this is the work of
women, maybe we should draft some
of ours into service.

OUEEN KRUSHAMEMNON enters the room.

QUEEN
I am ready to do battle. After bearing ten children for the king,
fighting the Athenians would be a
holiday. There is a rumor that many
races are led by female warriors.

This breaks the ice between the two Spartans and everyone enjoys a good laugh at this preposterous idea.

QUEEN
(Continuing) Are you finished thrashing out your differences like true
Spartan warriors or do you need more
bruises to impress the Roman ambassador who is waiting?

GEORGI
Our customs are slightly bruised
by such ridiculous ideas as women
warriors, but have quickly recovered
at the hilarity of the radiant Queen
of the Spartan's sense of jest.

QUEEN
You deserve a promotion for this double
flattery, but since you are already commander of the Spartan forces, you will
have to settle for dinner. Now, will you
see the Roman ambassador who is a rogue
among rogues, from what I hear?

GEORGI
The Roman pipsqueak can wait until
the river STYNX freezes over for all
I care. I want to continue this war
until Athens is destroyed, but the
king wants to make peace. May I be
so bold as to inquire what you, dear
Queen of Sparta, think of us quitting
the field when we have suffered
one small setback?

QUEEN
Would you have me answer as a women
or a Spartan?

GEORGI
Why not both?

QUEEN
All right. As a women and a mother,
I prefer to save youth for the couch,
even inferior Athenian youth. They
too have mothers who wait their return as I wait the return of my sons.
Alas, dear general, as a freedom
loving Spartan, I think they can
never be trusted to keep the peace.
They want to make the whole world
their servants. For this reason,
I would see them all in HADES tormented by the fiends of hell.

GEORGI
Well spoken, my Queen. I see I have an ally in the house of the king.

QUEEN
Are you then turning into a woman in your old age? I cannot make up my female mind whether I prefer to save them for the couch or the gods of the underworld.

KING KRUSH. laughs with gusto at the general's obvious discomfort at the Queen's ingenuous question.

GEORGI
Great gods! My Queen's tongue has been possessed by Zeus's fearsome thunderbolts.

KRUSH.
Ah, now I see the problem. Our armies have been defeated not by Athenian bravery, but by feminine indecision.

GEORGI
(Melting down and going ballistic big time, he attacks the king who hurls him over a couch) I will show you female indecision.

KRUSH.
Are you comfortable general? Have you forgotten who is king here? I was just joking or I would have had your head long before this. We've had enough fun for one day. There's a Roman ambassador to talk to. Send in the Roman spy.

QUEEN KRUSH. exists and MARCHELLO MACHIAVELLI enters.

MARCHELLO
Hail great King of the fierce Spartans.

KRUSH.
Hail rash spy of the malignant Romans.
What say you? It is a long time
since you paid us respects or what
is more important paid us for the
land you pave over with your roads.

MARCHELLO
I come under a flag of truce to offer
you goodwill from the Republic
of Rome.

GEORGI
How much gold have you brought us
Roman pipsqueak?

MARCHELLO
(Poor mouthing) I fear Rome is only
a small poor city of farmers
and road builders with many mouths
to feed. We seek only to trade in
peace with the Greeks and learn the
ways of the Spartans so that we
can defend our poor city in time
of war.

GEORGI
If you bring us no tribute, be gone
with you, before I hang you by
your flag of truce.
KRUSH.
Wait! I rule here ambassador. GEN-
ERAL GEORGIUSES forgets that some-
times.

MARCHELLO
(True sycophant) GENERAL GEORGIUSES!
It is indeed a great honor to meet
the world's greatest general. The
prowess and bravery of GENERAL
GEORGIUSES are feared the world over.

GEORGI
(Impressed) Where is your city again?
You say you build roads? I could
use some new roads.

KRUSH
They are a small city on a stream
called the Tiber. They got started as
grave diggers for the Etruscans.
Maybe you should put it on your
places to visit after we are finished
making peace with the Athenians.
They are a rude and savage bunch of
bumpkins. You might feel right at
home there.

MARCHELLO
The king makes many jests today.
As always, I am your grateful and
humble pupil. We Romans are much
slower than you Greeks. But we
are capable of learning, even malicious Athenian humor, which I can
see the king has been demonstrating
for our benefit. I have heard an
even funnier Athenian joke on the way
here. It is said that the mighty Sparta
wants to sue for peace with Athens after
one tiny defeat.

GEORGI
I like this man.

KRUSH.
Many times it has been said that the
Athenians were defeated, but this war
still rages after seven long years.
Soon there will not be a Greek alive
to instruct you barbarian animals in
the good manners expected of slaves.
To whose advantage can this be?

MARCHELLO
They are the richest city in the world.
With such power, they will soon be
instructing you in manners.

KRUSH.
They are one city against the combined
power of HELLAS.

MARCHELLO
They are determined to force their
customs on all the Hellions.

KRUSH
Are you censoring ATHENIAN customs?
You are both democracies. Why aren't
you praising their customs? You
should be great allies.

MARCHELLO
A republic like Rome hates a democracy like ATHENS. A republic is
a democracy in name only. It is a
very useful device to fool the poor
into thinking they are powerful.
It is the best way to keep their
loyalty until they are needed for war.
That is why we study Spartan customs.
We someday hope to have a king.

GEORGI
What need you of a king when soon
you will be Greek slaves? But tell
me, because I am not clear. What is
the difference between a republic
like Rome and a democracy like
ATHENS? Isn't it all mob rule?

MARCHELLO
A large difference. In a republic like Rome,
only people from the best families can
become senators and make laws. In a
democracy like ATHENS, any common
lout of a male citizen who gets up early
enough to take a seat in the amphitheater
before it fills up can vote on the laws
passed that day. It is true rule by the
ignorant mob. That is why you can't fail
to defeat them in this war. They do not
know from one day to the next what their
policies will be.

KRUSH
How does Rome keep from going broke
if it depends on the goodwill of
the mob for its power? The Athenian
louts empty their treasury by voting
themselves every luxury.

MARCHELLO
Our Roman senators only pretend to
love the mob. There is no waste of
money. We dole out just enough to
the poor to keep their months shut
and bodies strong enough to fight
our many wars. This is a form of
investment that pays many dividends
in the lives of the herd. The Athenians on the other hand allow their
mob to vote themselves jobs, educa-

tion and other luxuries that saps
the state of treasure. The worst
mistake is to give each man a job.
They begin to think they are kings
of their own country and will not
help the state unless they are deceived by their demagogue orators
into thinking it will benefit them
in some selfish way.

GEORGI.
This is indeed a dangerous form of
government that drains men from the
warrior pool.

KRUSH.
And men that have independent means
are arrogant and self loving. Not
fit to be ruled. Almost as bad as
nobles.

MARCHELLO
This is why we favor the Spartan
way of life. Such wildly conceived
ideas as Athenian democracy are a
menace to kings and republics alike.

CURTAIN /END ACT I/

CURTAIN/ACT II, SCENE I

ATLAS, son of KING KRUSHAMEMNON of Sparta, is sent with a letter from his father to JASON, Archon of the Athenians, who is his brother-in-law. A truce is in effect between Athens and Sparta for the purpose of holding peace talks after seven years of bloody warfare. The fighting up to now has mostly been between their allied vassal states and for this reason Athens and Sparta, which haven't suffered any irreparable damage hold no great enmity toward one another. This letter carried by ATLAS proposes the temple of DIANA, at Pylos, as the site of the forthcoming peace conference. ATLAS has heard of the beauty of LYSISTRATA and has a present for her, ostensibly from his father.

JASON
I shall prepare an immediate reply
to this proposal from the king your
father that the peace conference be
held at Pylos, at the temple of DIANA.
He is right that it is important
that we meet away from the cities
where our differences can be ironed
out without outside interference.
I just hope there isn't any problem
with that gossipy goddess who has
a bad reputation for meddling and even
worse things. At least we won't have the
demagogues to deal with.

ATLAS
Peace can never be achieved while it
is left to venal politicians. Most of them
are demagogues who speak for some party
that profits by war.

JASON
Wisely spoken, son of KRUSHAMEMNON.
While I go to my study to prepare
this letter, you will be entertained
by my daughter LYSISTRATA. She shall
receive your father's gift from your
own hands. I shall deliver his gift
to my wife myself.

ATLAS
I shall be honored great sir, although I am
not prepared to speak to a woman. We are
not allowed to speak to virgins in Sparta until
after we are married.

JASON
It is the opposite here. Let me advise you. I'm not sure there is any right way. No matter. You talk to them the same as you would a goddess. You give much flattery. Even more the clothes than themselves. Most importantly, be even more obsequious than a slave. And mind be cautious. They are even more capricious than the gods. (Speaks to his blue painted Celtic slave standing by) O'HARA, go fetch my daughter LYSISTRATA.

ATLAS
(After O'HARA exits) Where did you get such a weird looking savage?

JASON
He is of the savage barbarians known as Celt. They are a race that will never be civilized. They live on the edge of the world where we hunt them for sport.

Enter LYSISTRATA alone with a banzai tree in a pot.

JASON
What are you doing with that stunted tree my dear?

LYSISTRATA
It is a god my father. I pray to it. It's a gift from O'HARA.

JASON
I must speak to him. As though we already aren't overpopulated enough with sap filled gods on Olympus.

LYSISTRATA
But I love this little tree God father.

JASON
All right, but just don't start
painting yourself blue. Lysistrata,
my daughter, I present to you PRINCE
ATLAS, son of KRUSHAMEMNON,
King of the Spartans. You will honor
your father by entertaining the prince
until I return from writing a letter.
He has a gift for you... from his father.
I will return shortly

JASON & his slave O'HARA exit. ATLAS and LYSISTRATA are both tongue tied for a moment or two. They just stand and stare at one another stunned by the animal attraction they have toward one another.

ATLAS
(Very formally) To you LYSISTRATA,
daughter of JASON, great leader of
the Athenians, it is with the greatest
pleasure that I present this
small token of the deep affection
that the family of KRUSHAMEMNON
holds for the renowned family of
JASON and their divinely beautiful
daughter LYSISTRATA possessor of
clothes made by the hand of Athena herself.

LYSISTRATA
These rags. My maids cast offs. (Atlas addled)
I thought you Spartans hated us?

ATLAS
We do. Officially we hate you, but
unofficially we love you, because you
are fellow Greeks. We nobles
are above such petty squabbles.

You are my cousin after all.

LYSISTRATA
I don't hate you. You seem nice.

JASON
Take this gift. It is from my father.

LYSISTRATA
(Teasing) Oh... And I was hoping it
was from you.

ATLAS
(Dazed) Secretly it... You were? Do you get many
gifts from Athenian youths?

LYSISTRATA
I get a lot, but it is because they try to
please my father and get promotions.
They are terrible bores. They talk endlessly
of philosophy, a subject I dislike. I prefer
poets who rhyme about love.

ATLAS
You are honest.

LYSISTRATA
Worse. I am ingenuously frank. My
mother hates me for it. She punishes
me and gives me lessons in lying.
I refuse to listen. Lying is against
my nature. I love the truth.

ATLAS
Punishes you for telling the truth?
Is this the custom in Athens?

LYSISTRATA
It seems to be. The high priestess
of APOLLO thought me a naive little

fool for the same reason. So it
must be the custom of the whole world.

ATLAS
Yes. It is the same in Sparta. After
a time, one stops challenging authority.
They get so upset if you question the
most stupid things. It is considered to
be bad for military discipline.

LYSISTRATA
Have you killed many men?

ATLAS
(Youthful bravado) I have not been
sent into battle yet. But I am
looking forward to killing many
when I do.

LYSISTRATA
You may have to kill my father.

ATLAS
I would never be able to do so.

LYSISTRATA
What about your orders?

ATLAS
I would disobey them.

LYSISTRATA
Why don't you want to kill my father?
He is the enemy of Sparta.

ATLAS
I could not bear to have you hate
me.

LYSISTRATA
Am I any different than other people?

ATLAS
You are different than all other people.

LYSISTRATA
I have the same parts as your mother and your sister.

ATLAS
It is not the same. Sometimes when they make me angry, I almost hate them. I think some god has bewitched you. You smell so fresh and good like a freshly cut pine tree.

LYSISTRATA
I bath in pine scent.

ATLAS
Ah. Is that a new Athenian perfume?

LYSISTRATA
No, we use it to clean our floors actually. I use it as a scent because it is part of my religion. I am a tree worshipper.

ATLAS
I have heard of that. Isn't that a barbarian religion?

LYSISTRATA
Yes, but soon I will plant my god on Mt. Olympus and he will be the one supreme god.

ATLAS
I see. And you are enchanted by
this tree god?

LYSISTRATA
I am a devotee by choice. But are
you not ensnared in some gods net?
I have this strange feeling of
enchantment about you.

ATLAS
Is it not like anything you've ever
felt before?

LYSISTRATA
Sometimes when I secretly watch the
men wrestle, I have a strange enchanted feeling like I too want to
wrestle. It is the way I feel now.

ATLAS
You want to wrestle?

LYSISTRATA
Yes. But women are not allowed.
Do you feel like wrestling with me?

ATLAS
Yes. No. It is forbidden. Besides
I feel a little feverish.

LYSISTRATA
I too feel overly warm. Maybe I have
caught this enchanted fever from you.
Are you sick?

ATLAS
You have caught this sickness from me
and I from you.

LYSISTRATA
(Becoming frightened) Many people
in Athens die from the fever.
Will we die?

ATLAS
People seldom die of this fever.
It is called the fever of love.

LYSISTRATA
Love! What the poets waste so many
words on? Is it so? Can love be
a fever? My mother says poets are
dirty crazy dogs.

ATLAS
Your mother is right. This fever does
cause madness. Almost as bad as when
dogs foam at the mouth. But, oh what
sweet madness it is.

LYSISTRATA
It is true. Oh sweet madness that
is confusing my thoughts. I am helpless against this poet's madness. It
overcomes my senses and my sense. I
love you ATLAS, son of
KRUSHAMEMNON. What should I do?

ATLAS
You shall marry me.

LYSISTRATA
That is impossible. Our countries
are at war.

ATLAS
My father intends to make peace with
Athens and end this senseless war.
Then we can be married.

LYSISTRATA
My father has the same wish. He says peace is the only hope to save civilization from beasts like our slave O'HARA. Actually, O'HARA is very nice.

ATLAS
How then can peace fail? If the two most powerful men in the world want peace, how can any force in the world prevent it? There are many politicians who will speak against it, but my father and your father are the leaders of our people and cannot fail. Don't worry dear LYSISTRATA. We will soon be enjoying wedded bliss.

LYSISTRATA
If peace does fail, I will die rather than live without you.

ATLAS
If peace fails, I too will die rather than live without you. We shall be together always. Even in death.

O'HARA returns, overhears the last and announces to them that JASON is coming with the letter.

O'HARA
Take care young love. The patriarch returns

JASON
I hope you two have managed to find something to talk about in my absence (Gives ATLAS a letter to his father) For your father and it has been a pleasure to meet his handsome son. I hope you will honor my house

again with a visit when our countries are at peace. And that will be soon I think.

                    ATLAS
I pray the gods this may come about soon, as you say, honored sir. Until such time, may the gods keep you and your family from any harm. Good-bye fair LYSISTRATA.

They gaze longingly at one another as ATLAS exists.

                    JASON
A successfully negotiated pact methinks.

                    LYSISTRATA
Did you say something father?

                    JASON
No. I was just hoping out loud.

                    LYSISTRATA
I love you daddy.

CURTAIN
END OF ACT II, SCENE I

CURTAIN
ACT II, SCENE II

This scene takes place at the AGORA (Marketplace) in Athens. The populace is about evenly divided over what course of action to pursue against Sparta. It is the first military advantage the Athenians have had over the Spartans in the seven years of constant warfare and there is a strong desire to take sweet revenge for all the misery suffered at their hands. There are two factions that dominate: the hawks who want war to continue and the doves who favor peace. The hawks have as their champion the orator BARRY MAD CAL PANASSES, JR. The spokesman for the dovish faction is the orator DIODOTES.

DIODOTES is supported in the great debate by the philosopher SOCRATES, the writer of comedies ARISTOPHENES and the spice merchant CURITHIAS. DIODOTUS' speech brings about sympathy for peace. BARRY PANASSESES previous entourage in SCENE I Act I plus STOOLITES, the dung collector, support him. BARRY, whose speech favoring war is not well received, predicts that his rhetoric will win in the end.

                SOCRATES
Not being a man of great wit, I must say
bluntly that MAD CAL must be stopped
by any means short of assassination. He
will be the death of Athens if his ideas
prevail.

                DIODOTUS
I too am a man of little wit SOCRATES.
I have been laughing at his mad popu-
list ravings for years. It is incon-
ceivable that such a mad jerk could
be taken seriously. But he is becoming more popular with the mob with
each passing day.

                SOCRATES
He will tell the mob anything it wants
to hear to win its favor.

                ARISTOPHENES
I have poked fun at all the world,
including you gentleman, but even I
am sobered by this monster. Sparta
is offering to accept the humilia-
tion of making peace, but all is to
be doomed by those few who profit
from war.

                SOCRATES
Perhaps we are the mad ones hoping
to make the mob listen to reason

when they are ruled from birth to
death by their foolish desires

ARISTOPHENES
As the world turns, and of that no man
is certain, except me, men of peace are
to men of war, what a fart is in the middle
of lovemaking.

DIODOTUS
Or a belch in the middle of gluttony. The
indigestion of nations is caused by power
and domination. And Athens has a great
appetite.

SOCRATES
Then the skills of a demagogue are
the same as those of a great chef?
He tempts people with tantalizingly
irresistible ideas spiced with every
conceivable intellectual condiment.
Food for fools.

ARISTOPHENES
Such food is nothing, but dung masked
by a lot of harmful spices that will
probably kill you and make you food
for the worms.

SOCRATES
I must admit a weakness for spices.
Spices are useful if used properly.
It is the chef that is bad. And in
the case of Barry, the chef is mad.
That is why they call him MAD CAL.
His very breath poisons the mind.

DIODOTUS
If he wins over the mob, he'll bray

until we are exiled to the wild kingdom. You ARISTOPHENES will have to write plays to amuse the beasts of the field while SOCRATES must butt heads philosophically with the goats and I will be left to make speeches to the birds.

SOCRATES
If I may indulge myself with one of my philosophical riddles, may I ask why a man of virtue would not benefit by going to a butcher to have a splinter removed from his finger?

ARISTOPHENES
The butcher in this case would hack off the finger to cure the splinter and then sell the finger as a fine cut of meat.

SOCRATES
Which might be beneficial to the man of virtue who would not be so gullible the next time. The reason it is bad is that if you give a butcher one finger, he will next take your whole arm.

DIODOTUS
But harming his fellow citizens is not to his advantage is it?

SOCRATES
A butcher does not have a concern for the animal he is slaughtering; only the price of meat. He is blind to the suffering of others.

DIODOTUS
Then the evil of the demagogue is
to put self interest above all other interests?

SOCRATES
This is always the case DIODOTUS.

ARISTOPHENES
Sometimes they have good intentions,
but shallowness of understanding
makes them men of fast action and
brash deeds.

SOCRATES
This shallowness must inevitably
lead to grave error as sooner or
later, he must use his own judgment.
A city would be in grave peril with
such a man at the reins.

DIODOTUS
Right Socrates. He is more a fool
than a scoundrel. His popular
ideas bring him many followers, but
his mistakes cause him to become a
tyrant.

SOCRATES
Yes. He hides his mistakes by re-
moving the heads of his detractors.

ARISTOPHENES
Then the fool is worse than the
scoundrel

SOCRATES
Demagogues are both. Their
object is to fool the gullible into
being supporters of their dangerous
schemes. He is the court jester of the
mob.

ARISTOPHENES
Then evil wears a clown suit. I must
be evil then, because I am a clown.

SOCRATES
The difference is you claim to be
a clown when you are really serious
and the demagogue pretends to be
serious when he is really a clown.

ARISTOPHENES
And sometimes the rascal even
manages a joke. What method can be
used to expose his folly?

DIODOTUS
With the help of your wisdom and wit,
I shall answer him issue for issue.

BARRY MAD CAL PANASSES and friends confront DIODOTUS and friends.

BARRY
What say you DIODOTUS? Are you for
pressing for our victory and the annihilation of our perennial foe?

DIODOTUS
Are you speaking of pressing the
great grape battle BARRY. It seems
a waste of time. Why press time of
its vintage waste when it does its
own work? If it is pressing lives
you speak of, let us do away with
waste, the worst part of lives.

BARRY
Hear this O men of Athens? A waste
of time to destroy our enemies.
Here is a man of waste STOOLITES,

collector of dung. What is your
opinion in this matter of wasting
lives?

STOOLITES
I love defecation as other men love
perfume who trade in perfume. I
love stools as other men love rare
spices. Any man who stands against
waste is against prosperity. I am
of MAD CAL'S party because he wants
to waste our enemies. Peace is a
waste of time.

ARISTOPHENES
We have a partnership between crap
and the pot. Why don't you call yourselves the party of crappots BARRY?

BARRY
None could be so foul as the crap you
write. Anyone who would write a
play called Peace, when we daily must
defend our lives against such peaceful
neighbors as we have must indeed
poison the very soil with his mad
stools. And what's worse, you misquote me.

ARISTOPHENES
You have never spoken twice the
same words, so to quote you is to
misquote you in advance. Here is a
great tragic actor. What is your opinion
sir actor?

ACTOR
I am against MAD CAL'S party of crappots because they do not support
public funding of tragedy.

BARRY
I beg your pardon sir. I am against
public aid to the indigent of all
kinds except the worthy, and as such,
I would favor giving to worthy causes such
as tragedy because tragedy like war is a
worthy cause. As long as public funds are
used to suppress unworthy causes such as
comedy, I am for it.

ACTOR
(Who is in tatters)? My profound apologies
great orator. Since it is the
untalented riff-raff comedians you scorn
in favor of aid to worthy tragedians I
should get enough to buy a pair of sandals.
You've won my vote great demagogue.

ARISTOPHENES
Indeed sir ham! One for and one against
makes twice the fool. He has two'd
your vote and won your wits.

BARRY
How shall you quote me on this issue
in your next play?

ARISTOPHENES
I shall say, quote, "I am against
all public aid except aid to my
friends".

GENERAL
You strumpet tongue from HADES,
have you no respect for fleecing the
mob to entertain the gods?

ARISTOPHENES
If by entertainment, you mean constant
warfare, robbery of children,

unrestrained greed, enslaving the
world to slave wages and rape of
defenseless sheep, I too am entertained, but it is stupid tragedy and I am
partial to comedy.

           GENERAL
Are you against democracy? Democracy
is self government. People are free
to vote. Are you a poor sport that
hates what the majority votes for?

         ARISTOPHENES
After the demagogues like BARRY
finish lying to them, they would
vote to have motherhood and apple pie
declared indecent.

          SOCRATES
Is not democracy the best form of government ever invented?

         ARISTOPHENES
It hasn't been invented yet. That
is the problem.

          SOCRATES
Then what we call democracy is not
democracy?

         ARISTOPHENES
Democracy is anything you want to
call it. The Spartans who hold
all goods in common claim to be
democrats because their nobles make
their laws.

           GENERAL
BARRY is a true democrat.

ARISTOPHENES
If you mean catering to the needs
of dung collectors, ham actors, war
loving generals, builders of public
buildings, arms merchants, casket
makers, foreign governments or anybody else that contributes money to
buy his vote, I agree he is a democrat.

BARRY
So why do you hate democracy so much?
We provide jobs for the rich and the
rich provide scraps for the poor.
Is this not better than letting everyone
go hungry?

ARISTOPHENES
The definition of Democracy is not beggar.
Until there is a law that guarantees every
citizen the dignity of a job, there can be no
democracy, only pseudo-democracy.

SOCRATES
At least we have pseudo-democracy in
Athens. That is better than no
democracy at all.

DIODOTUS
Pseudo-democracy? That's a fool's
democracy.

BARRY
You see idealistic young fool. Even
the great SOCRATES agrees that a
system of government based on predatory greed is no worse for being
a fool's democracy. Take from others
the way they would take from you if
they had the chance. This is Athenian

wit admired by all the world.

DIODOTUS
What you call democracy is the rule
of the jungle. A democracy is only
as good as its poorest citizen.

ORACALLIS
A part of democracy is better than
the whole of despotism. Vote for
BARRY for Archon and he will put a
goose in every pot.

ARISTOPHENES
You got your goose where your head
belongs.

SOCRATES
These crappotters want to cook Athens
goose by skewering its youth in war.

BARRY
Nations like men must strive for wealth
or die in poverty. War is as necessary as
air or water.

DIODOTUS
Do you hear men of Athens? You must
eat drink and breath war. Stoolites?
What say you now dung buyer.

STOOLITES
It makes sense. My sons will go and
fight so that the dung business doesn't die.
I will be rich when we crapture new cities.

DIODOTUS
If anybody is left alive to fill the
crappers. CURITHIAS! Sir spice

shipper. Who will you back?

CURITHIAS
I am for you. BARRY will ruin business.

BARRY
How now! You disagree with others of business?

CURITHIAS
Indeed. Who can afford small luxuries like spices when you tax us so heavily to pay for your wars? War is only profitable to orators and arms shippers. The rest of us have to pay with our lives and fortunes. Give me a job and peace so that I will be able to afford a small luxury or two.

BARRY
Bah. Peace is a lemon. It brings poverty to everyone but spice dealers.

DIODOTUS
What war have we profited by?

BARRY
Troy brought us much gold; enough to build this modern city.

DIODOTUS
That is a lie. The only gold we got from Troy were a few gold teeth. And your ancestors were Trojan slaves; a small gain indeed.

BARRY
The Spartans stole it out from under the nose of the Athenian commander.

And that dunce was your ancestor.
We will have all the gold in the
world after we destroy Sparta.

DIODOTUS
Lies, lies, lies...

Friends of BARRY start a chant of BARRY, BARRY, BARRY, GOLD, GOLD, SPEECH, SPEECH, SPEECH. BARRY takes his place on the hustings, called the bema in those times and makes a lengthy and emotional speech appealing for war to the end against the Spartans.

BARRY
I have observed again that a democracy such as ours cannot exist and
lead the world by being afraid to
accept responsibility. The case of
this small island of SPHAGIAE filled
with hostile forces under imminent
danger of destruction by our own
forces is another example of your
weakness and folly. You have yielded
your pity on the principle of merciful humanity. By allowing their existence you are now guilty of open
weakness, dangerous to your own existence. Your thanks for your kindness will be a knife in the back at
the first opportunity. You should
remember that our own economic existence is a despotism exercised
over unwilling subjects, who are
conspiring against you: they do not
allow your exploitation in return
for any kindness you do them to
your own injury. Their friendship
is based on your own omnipotence.
You are their masters. They have
no love for you and would gladly

take your place had they your power.
We forget that a state in which laws,
though imperfect, are productive,
is better off than one in which laws
are good but powerless. Let us not
then perfect our laws to the point
at which we are so full of humanity
that the leading individuals cannot
act. Soon slavery would be abolish-
ed by such an immoderate good. May
the gods protect Athens from such do
gooders. Ignorance and self control
is a more useful combination than
cleverness and license; and the more
simple sort generally make better
citizens than the more astute. I
pride myself on being a simple man
of the people. The astute desire
to be thought wiser than the laws.
They want to be always taking the
lead in the discussion at the assembly; they think that they can nowhere have finer opportunity of
speaking their mind, and their folly
usually results in the ruin of their
country; whereas the dull sort, mis-
trusting their own capacity, admit
that the laws are wiser than themselves. They do not have preten-
sions of being able to criticize
the arguments of a great speaker.
And being impartial judges, not am-
bitious rivals, these dull minds
are usually in the right. That is
the spirit in which we should act;
not suffering ourselves to be so
excited by our own cleverness in a
war of wits as to advise the Athenian
people contrary to our own better

judgment. The question of war or peace is before the Athenian people. I myself have not changed in my feelings toward the Spartans. Any change is to the benefit of the evildoer. Your anger waxes dull and you forget the issues at stake in this great fight, only remembering your pleasure in places no longer accessible. Now as victor, you would throw away your chance of victory when you could easily destroy this trapped army and push the murderers of your sons back to their own walls. Only a democracy would throw away such an opportunity to exact just revenge. What tyrant would suffer such abuse at the hands of a defeated foe? And again I wonder whom will answer me, and whether he will attempt to show that the crimes of the men on this island are a benefit to us, or that when we suffer, our allies suffer with us. Clearly he must be someone who has such confidence in his powers of speech as to contend that you never can make up your own minds. Or else he is one of the enemy or in their pay and under this apostasy seeks to befuddle you by sophisticated speech and thus divert you from your resolve. In such speech contests as this you decide the fate of your city. You are to blame for listening politely to such traitorous speeches without severely punishing the culprit. You estimate the possibility of future enterprises from the eloquence of an orator. Simple fact proposed by

simple men like myself falls on deaf
ears. No men, beside yourselves,
are more quickly duped or sooner deceived by novel notions, or on the
contrary are slower to follow fact-
ual advice such as mine. You despise
what is familiar to glorify the
novel. In a word, you are at the
mercy of your own ears, and sit like
spectators attending a performance
of actors, but very unlike counselors
of state. I want to put aside this trifling,
and therefore say to you that no
single city has ever injured us so
deeply as has Sparta. They seek
to perpetuate ideals that can never
be adjusted to our own. They challenge us in every country of our
influence. They undermine our
authority and seek to cause revolt
of those whom we dominate. Yet
in our hour of strength, you would
give them sustenance and allow them
to exist like a tumor in our breast.
I say punish them as they would you.
In one word, if you do as I say, you
will do what is just to the Spartans,
(Howls of laughter) and also what is
expedient for yourselves. For if they
were right in starting this war, you must
be wrong in maintaining your democratic
institutions. Mercy should be shown to
the merciful and not thrown away on the
merciless that by force of circumstances
must always be our enemies. Do not be
soft hearted at their present distress, but
remember your sons who they have
put to death. Crush this cruel foe
once and for all and be true to the
purpose of those who have died that

you may live in freedom.

There is much cheering at the end of the speech. BARRY leaves the BEMA smiling and shaking hands with seemingly everyone in the crowd. This has been a highly emotional speech. In sharp contrast, he is followed on the hustings by the noble and dignified DIODOTUS who speaks in a calm but forceful manner. BARRY'S followers roundly boo him before he can begin. There are shouts of traitor, villain and other epithets. One man draws a sword, but is restrained by the friendly spice merchant who throws pepper in his eyes.

                CURITHIAS
        Athens is a democracy and every man
        has a right to speak his piece.
        Any man who doubts this can taste my
        pepper in his eyes, free of charge.

The crowd settles down and allows DIODOTUS to begin his speech.

                DIODOTUS
        I am far from blaming those who in-
        vite us to reconsider our resolve
        to attack the island of Sphagiae,
        nor do I approve of the censure
        that has been cast on the practice
        of deliberating freely in the public
        forum about matters so critical.
        In my opinion, the two things most
        adverse to good counsel are haste
        and passion; the former is generally
        a mark of folly, the latter of vul-
        garity and narrowness of mind. When
        a man insists that words ought not
        be our guides in action, he is either
        wanting in sense, if he does not see
        that there is no other way in which
        we can throw light on the unknown
        future; or he is not honest if, seek-
        ing to carry a discreditable measure,
        and knowing he cannot speak well in

a bad cause, he reflects that he can slander well and terrify his opponents with the audaciousness of his calumnies. Worst of all are those who, besides other topics of abuse, declare that their opponent is hired, against the best interest of Athens, to make an eloquent speech. If they accused him of stupidity only, when he failed in making an impression, he might go his way having lost his reputation for good sense but not for honesty; whereas he who is accused of dishonesty, even if he succeed, is viewed with suspicion, and if he fail, is thought to be both fool and rogue. And so the city suffers; for she is robbed of her counselors by fear. The good citizen should prove his superiority as a speaker by not trying to intimidate those who will follow him in debate except by fair argument; and the wise city ought not to give increased honor to her best counselor, any more than she will deprive him of that which he has; while he whose proposal is rejected not only ought to receive no punishment, but should be free from all reproach. Then he who succeeds will not say pleasant things contrary to his better judgment in order to gain a still higher place in popular favor, and he who fails will not strive to attract the multitude to himself by like compliances. But we take an opposite course, and when the best advice is offered in plain terms, it is as much distrusted as the worst; and not only he who wishes

to lead the multitude into the most
dangerous courses must deceive you,
but he who speaks in the cause of
right must himself lie and exaggerate
to gain the support of the masses.
Thus the fool in his quest for pop-
ularity has forced the wise to play
the fool in order to save you from
your own folly that would lead to
your destruction. How has such a
tragic state of affairs overtaken
us at the height of our glory? The
answer is simple. We have let the
community spirit of our forefathers
be undermined by self-interest.
I do not come forward either as an
advocate of the enemy or as their
accuser; the question for us, right-
ly considered, is not, what are
their crimes but what is for our
interest? If I prove them ever so
guilty, I will not, on that account
bid you put them to death, unless
it is useful. Neither, if perchance
there be some degree of excuse for
them, would I have you spare them,
unless it is clearly for the good
of the state. For I conceive that
we are now concerned not with the
present, but with the future. When
my adversary PANASSES, insists that
the infliction of their destruction
will be expedient and will secure
you against their continued encroach-
ment in time to come, I like him,
taking the ground of future useful-
ness of such action by us, stoutly
maintain that expediency will have the
opposite effect; I cannot in good
conscience have you misled by the

apparent fairness of his proposal,
and thus reject the solid advantages to be gained by the opposite.
You are angry with the Spartans,
and the unquestioned superior justice
of his argument may for the moment
attract you; however, you should
consider that justice is not on trial
as he would have you believe and we
are not in lawsuit with them, and do
not want to be told what is just;
we are considering a matter of policy, and desire to know how we can
turn it to our greatest future advantage. Consider also that we are
opposed by conflicting ideals and
that PANASSES would have us destroy
an idea by destroying a few enemy
soldiers. This seems to be the
height of folly. An idea can only
be supplanted by the birth of a
better idea. To many offenses less
than theirs, states have affixed
the punishment of death; nevertheless, excited by hope or necessity,
men still risk their lives. None
when venturing on a perilous enterprise yet passed a sentence of
failure on himself. And what city
acting as one mind ever imagined
that the power which she had, did
not justify the war she pursued.
All living beings are by nature
prone to err both in public and
in private life, and no law will
prevent them from such error.
Men have gone through the whole
catalog of penalties in the hope
that, by increasing their severity,
they may suffer less at the hands

of evildoers. And still there are
transgressors. Some greater terror
then has yet to be discovered; certainly death deters no one. For
poverty inspires necessity with dar-
ing and wealth engenders avarice with
pride and insolence; thus the various passions of human life lure men
to destruction; and states even more
than individuals, because they are
gambling for higher stakes; freedom
or slavery. In a word, then, it is
impossible that human nature when
pressed by necessity or passion can
be restrained by the power of law
or any other terror. We ought then,
not act hastily out of a mistaken
reliance on the security which the
penalty of destruction offers.
Be assured then that what I advise
is for the best, and yielding neither
to pity nor to leniency, for I am
as unwilling as BARRY to admit any
justice in their actions, but simply
weighing the arguments which I have
urged, offer them the hand of friendship they ask. Then set about im-
proving your own great ideas and
change the course of all history by
proving that all men should have an
opportunity to live free of undo
need and tyrannical greed. If you
destroy the people on this island,
you will not destroy the thoughts
of our despotism or the poverty of
the world. We should assure them
of the intractability of our inhumanity and the justice of their
cause. I call on you, men of Athens,
to lose an island and gain the re-

spect of the world.

There is tumultuous cheering. Many of the same people who booed DIODOTUS now cheer him and shake his hands. Such is the power of orators to sway the masses. There is a chant of "peace" and BARRY and his entourage hastily depart. DIODOTUS' oration has carried the day.

>BARRY
>Let us depart my friends and live
>to win another day.

CURTAINS
ACT II, SCENE II

ACT II, SCENE III

LYSISTRATA and ATLAS are seen in a secluded spot in a forest. There is a shrine to DIANA near by. They are married by a druid Celtic priest O'HARA, who is also the Celtic slave of JASON. If the war continues, they all plan to run away to the land of the Celts (Ireland) where O'HARA is from. Their faces are painted blue. When DIANA and MACHIAVELLI show up, and see people with blue faces, DIANA thinks aliens have invaded her shrine.

>O'HARA
>This shrine of DIANA seems like as
>good a spot as any.

>LYSISTRATA
>I know the gods and goddesses of
>Olympus are just an invention of
>some poet's fevered imagination,
>but don't you think it's a little
>brassy using DIANA'S shrine to get
>married in? She's a terrible gossip.

>O'HARA
>Trust me. There's only one God and
>He's a tree.

There is a rumble of thunder.

                    ATLAS
        That sounded like father ZEUS. You
        better be careful of what you say or
        he may turn us all into burning
        bushes.

                    O'HARA
        (Slightly shaken) It sounds like a rain-
        storm to me. Forget these silly super-
        stitions and let's get on with this druid
        wedding ceremony. Hold hands children.

                    LYSISTRATA
        We need witnesses. ZEUS must have
        frightened ours off.

DIANA now shows up hand in hand with MARCHELLO MACHIAVELLI who is
dressed as Apollo.

                    DIANA
        My, my APOLLO. It seems my house
        has been invaded by blasphemous aliens.
        We will have to scare them away.
        All humans are terrified of gods.

                    O'HARA
        You there. Who are you?

                    DIANA
        I am DIANA and this is Apollo.

                    O'HARA
        Yes. And I am ZEUS disguised as a
        druid priest.

                    LYSISTRATA
        (To Apollo) Haven't we met before

father Apollo? You look a lot
like the Roman ambassador.

MARCHELLO
You're mistaken my dear. He looks
like me.

DIANA
(Furious) You dare insult the gods
you pipsqueak mortals? How would
you like to boil in Hades forever?

O'HARA
(Cutting her off) And how would you
like to be witnesses at a Celtic
wedding ceremony officiated by a
druid priest of the one true tree God?

DIANA
I only allow bi-sexual weddings at my
shrine.

MARCELLO (APOLLO)
She'll do it this time if you promise to not
tell anyone you saw the two of us together.

O'HARA
Why? Are you ashamed of being with heteros?
Come children. Take each other's hands,
we have witnesses, even if thy are perverts.

LYSISTRATA and JASON take each other's hands as instructed. Everyone seems a little spooked by the situation except O'HARA, firm in his belief in his god.

O'HARA
Do you ATLAS, son of KRUSHAMEMNON,
take LYSISTRATA, daughter of JASON,
to be your tree hugging wedded wife and to

have and to hold her in as much esteem in sickness
and health as you do a giant cedar of Lebanon?

                ATLAS
I do.

                O'HARA
And do you LYSISTRATA take this man
ATLAS to be your duly wedded husband
and agree to forgive him when he gets
drunk and beats you?

              LYSISTRATA
I do if that's an important celtic custom.

                O'HARA
Then, in the name of the leaf, the
tree, and the holy trunk, I pronounce
you man and wife and Celts. You may
kiss the bride.

ATLAS and LYSISTRATA kiss. DIANA and MACHIAVELLI shake hands and exit into the temple.

                O'HARA
Ha, ha. DIANA and APOLLO. People
are so gullible. They will believe anything. Here is a bottle of Woad my dears.
It's blue paint. On proper occasions, you
put it on to show that you are Celts.

              LYSISTRATA
I don't mind the blue faces and
worshipping trees, but must I encour-
age my husband to get drunk and
beat me?

                O'HARA
It is our religion. We believe the

man should wear the skirt in the
family.

LYSISTRATA
This is barbarism at its worst, but
I will endure any indignity to escape these endless Greek wars. Where
is the land of your Celts?

O'HARA
It is an isle far to the west known
as the emerald isle.

ATLAS
How will we find our way to such a
distant and strange land?

O'HARA
We shall steal a boat and sail to
the west until we pass the Pillars
of Hercules; then we shall sail north
careful to follow our nose after
that. If it smells all flowery and
nice, it is a Gaulful place inhabited
by gluttoness gourmands who wear
scents of flowers to hide their corruption.
When there is the scent in the air
of sulfurous cabbage, you will know
you have arrived at my exotic homeland, the sweetest smelling place
in the world.

LYSISTRATA
You sure it isn't the smell of un-
bathed bodies.

O'HARA
That too, but after you've had a
couple of pints of our stout you
won't notice it much.

ATLAS
(Condescending) It sounds like a
fine place. If the peace talks
fail, we will all escape there together.

O'HARA
The peace talks will fail. Mark
my word.

ATLAS
But DIODOTUS won the vote of confidence in the debate. And JASON and
my father are for peace. How can
peace fail?

O'HARA
There will be another debate. And
the gods only know the outcome. The
fickle Athenians are the most inconstant of lovers.

LYSISTRATA
Then we must be prepared to fly or
die. We would be put to death if
our marriage was to become known.

ATLAS
We may anyway if it becomes known
that we are converted to tree worshippers.

LYSISTRATA
But don't you think it is better
to worship one god you can see and
touch than a whole lot of drunken
sots no one has ever seen?

O'HARA
There is only one God and his spirit
is in every tree.

ATLAS
When I was on the way here and hid
in a pasture during the day, I saw
a god that looked just like the one
who was just here and he was trying
to mount a sheep from behind.

O'HARA
How do you know it was not a Sheppard?

ATLAS
Because he was dressed as APOLLO,
claimed to be APOLLO, and spoke Latin,
which he said was the language of APOLLO.

O'HARA
That is a trick used by Roman spies
to tempt Greeks into doing their
will.

ATLAS
A Roman spy?

LYSISTRATA
Never mind my dear. Now you are
mine and we will worship the one
true God who will protect us from
such perverts.

O'HARA
I must be going back or I will be missed.

Exit O'HARA. ATLAS and LYSISTRATA immediately embrace.

ATLAS
I will die rather then ever be parted
from you again. We must escape.

LYSISTRATA
Have no fear my dear. The Trees

will be with us. I love you husband.

                    ATLAS
I love you wife.

                CURTAINS
                ACT II, SCENE III

                ACT II, SCENE IV

Same as Act I, Scene I. DIANA, the scantily clad HUNTRESS, with bow and quiver over shoulder is serving the same group. She is speaking to the Eye of Zeus stealth TV camera at the rise.

                    DIANA
Here we are Gods And Goddesses,
back eavesdropping on
the kind of mortals that make the
eternally boring lives of the gods
bearable. This is a group that is
roundly depressed over what seems
to be inevitable peace between Athens
and Sparta. We must do everything
in our power, short of actually
helping them, to find some way to
stop this peace catastrophe. I also have
some other bad news. There is a
dangerous heresy afoot to replace
us with the worship of one god.
Who but a Celt would start a religeon that believes God is a tree?
And the simple-minded convert daughter
of Archon Jason wants to plant
her God right on Mt. Olympus.
As though we don't have enough trees
and gods on Olympus. Wait till ZEUS
hears. He'll light up her life the
next time she takes shelter under her

God in a rainstorm. There is thick
plotting going on here. Let's listen
in for some spicy tid bits.

BARRY
Do not fret my friends. The Athenians are the most whimsical of
lovers. DIODOTUS may have won their
applause last week, but I shall win
their vote this week. We need only
come up with a seductive enough plot
and in spite of all his appeal to the
rational side of man, a proper stew
of emotions will always win in the
end over wisdom and reason. Such
is the cupidity of men. Here is a
drachma, ORICALLIS. Cheer us up
and tell us who is going to win the
great debate.

ORICALLIS
You will be the victor in this final
debate, because the Athenians never
vote the same way twice.

BARRY
Now you know why I let DIODOTUS
win the last debate. He will be
ostracized after my speech this
week. I promise you.

HERCULES
What good will it do us? The following week, the inconstant Athenians
will ostracize you and we will be
back where we started.

BARRY
I will see to it that there are no
more speeches by anybody after

this week. It will be war, war,
war until every last Spartan is
dead. So stop thinking about all
the money you're going to make
long enough to come up with something to tell the Athenians that
will get their attention.

> HERCULES

I sponsor public events. I bribe
your followers. I finance your
think tank. What are they thinking
about if they have no ideas? You
want me to do your thinking for you
too? What am I getting for my money?

> BARRY

Don't be so quick to offense.

> HERCULES

Then why do you cast slurs on my
money?

> BARRY

You take the wrong meaning from my
words. Perhaps you are guilty
about the blood on your money?

> HERCULES

There! Now it is blood money.

> BARRY

Again, no harm meant. I don't care
if you destroy all the youth of the
world with your arms. I just want
to find a way to help you.

DIANA
(As serving boy) Hooray!

BARRY
You see HERCULES? I have made you one convert already.

HERCULES
A boy like that knows nothing of politics.

BARRY
All Greeks know politics. Let us question him. Boy, boy. Serving boy.

DIANA
(Drunk checking herself out) Yes, master. I am a boy. Is there something, something you need that only a boy can give?

BARRY
I would not what a girl could give fool. I want to ask of you some political advice.

DIANA
(Relieved) Right manly politics I thrive on sir. What is it you want to know sir?

BARRY
How think you about war or peace with the Spartan beasts?

DIANA
Methinks I will vote with the gods for war.

BARRY
How now, that's a smart lad. But
Athens is about to snatch defeat
from the jaws of victory. The
folly prone Athenians are determined to have peace. I must talk
them out of it, but I have no plan.

DIANA
You must convince them that war is
peace. It is done all the time.
If you could only see the future
like us... (ZEUS fires off a warning
thunderbolt) Whoops! I made a boo
boo. (She jumps on a pedestal and
resumes being Diana)

BARRY
Disappeared into thin air. Must
have been some god in disguise, but
he gave me a great idea.

GENERAL
It better be better than your last
one.

BARRY
If you would use your head for something better than a brush, I might
not have to do all the thinking.

GENERAL
Boy, boy, where is that confounded
boy. (Diana springs into action)
Give me more wine.

BARRY has already forgotten that it was the boy's idea and not his own. So has everyone else.

HERCULES
Then tell us your big idea. We pay

you well to come up with grandiose
schemes to fool the masses. I even
heard a rumor the Romans have hired
you to draw up a plan of world
conquest.

BARRY
I don't believe in putting all my
eggs in one basket any more than
you do mister leading arms supplier
to the whole world. As for my
plan, it can't fail. I am going
to convince even the most liberal
humanitarian Athenian that death
is the greatest favor we can bestow
on the Spartans.

GENERAL
I think we have heard that plan somewhere before. Boy! More wine.

DIANA pours the wine & borrows the general's helmet.

DIANA
(Drunk) We shall have war, glorious
war.

BARRY
(Giving him a coin) ORACALLIS. Tell
these doubters what the fortune of
my new plan will be.

ORACALLIS
(Concentrating) I see a great multitude cheering for war. Athens
will attack the Spartans and destroy
them and BARRY will become dictator.

ALL
Long live BARRY! Tyrant of Athens!

BARRY
(Ecstatic) I shall be tyrant of Athens.

HERCULES
You shall be opposed. This is a democracy.

BARRY
I will be the first tyrant in history to convince the masses that this is a democracy when it is really a dictatorship.

ORACALLIS
But not the last.

DIANA
I'll drink to that. There'll never be a real democracy.

ZEUS is really pissed. He hurls another thunderbolt and hits Diana in the butt.

ZEUS

"Women! Never trust them with a secret".

HERCULES
The state needs tax money for arms. That is why democracy is good. People pay a lot of taxes. And I get rich.

BARRY
Don't worry. I'll protect democracy to the last drop of its money.

GENERAL
I need weapons. (Glaring at HERCULES) Weapons that don't fall apart.

BARRY
Don't worry. I have a secret weapon.
(To general) Draft the spice merchant
and put him in the front line.

ORACALLIS
Barry has a secret weapon. Democracy
is safe.

BARRY
Democracy is safe. I have a secret
weapon. I will be the first tyrant to
pretend to be a democrat.

ORACALLIS
But not the last.

ALL
(Toast) Democracy is safe. Barry
will be tyrant. Hooray for tyrants.

DIANA
Hooray for tyrants.

ZEUS goes ballistic as the curtain comes down.

CURTAINS
ACT II, SCENE IV

ACT III, SCENE I

The temple of DIANA near Pylos. JASON, head of the Athenian state is meeting with KING KRUSHAMEMNON, head of the Spartan state in a peace meeting. They dismiss their followers and decide to meet alone. They have known each other since boyhood and are related by marriage.

JASON
I take it as a personal failure that

this war has befallen our peoples.
If it is not soon ended, our great
civilization will fail and the barbarians will fall on us showing us
no mercy. But first let us be re-
acquainted before we get to such
weighty matters.

                KING

Why don't we skip the pleasantries.
I want you to know at the outset
how sorrowfully I feel the pain of
the hostilities that exist between
our two great cities. I attempted
at the beginning to forestall the
young war hawks, but my voice went
unheeded. Now many of them are dead
so my task is a lighter one but still
difficult. This meeting, while sanctioned
by the nobles is still held in abhorrence
by many and the proceedings will be
subject to ratification by the leadership
counsel. The age of kings is dead. The
mob rules.

                JASON

We leading men of Athens have the
same problem. There is even talk
of choosing a leader who comes
from the common herd. He is known
as BARRY PANASSES, JR. son of
MAD CAL PANASSES, SR., the ass
breeder. He is just like his father, such a
stubborn fool, the stubborn animals
they breed have been named after
them. He attended one of our many
popular schools of sophistry where they
teach the sons of fools rhetoric,
which is the art of pleasantly lying.
Now he persists in every wild cause

that will fire the mob into making
him their hero. Surely ZEUS has sent
him among us to scourge us for some
obscure slight.

              KING

I have heard of the man. The Spartans
consider him less a stubborn fool
than a madman. We call him by his
father's name MAD COW, because of
his mad claims like claiming men
will some day jump over the moon
like a cow on loco weed. They even say
his father has become a god and the
moon is his domain. He is stubborn
in his hatred of Sparta too. If he
becomes ARCHON, it will be war until
one side or the other is destroyed.

              JASON

That is why we must find a way for
peace to work. The forces of destruction grow stronger by the day.

              KING

I have a proclamation to read to you
from the Lacedaemonian people and
then we can bargain on the terms for
peace. If this is agreeable to you?

              JASON

Read ahead. Knowing your manners,
it must be very brief, like throw
down your arms or we'll tear them
off. (They both have a laugh)

              KING

The Spartans invite you to make

terms with them and to finish the war. They offer peace and alliance and a general friendly and happy relation, and they ask in return that you do not destroy the people of the island of Sphagiae whom you have in your power. Now, if ever, is the time of reconciliation for us both, before either has suffered any irremediable calamity, which must cause, besides the ordinary antagonism of contending states, a personal and inveterate hatred, that will deprive you of the advantages which we now offer you. While the contest is still undecided, while you may acquire reputation and our friendship, and while our disaster can be prevented on tolerable terms, and disgrace be averted, let us be reconciled, and choosing peace instead of war ourselves, let us give relief and rest to all the Hellenes. The chief credit of the peace will be yours. Whether you or we have caused the world to be in a state of turmoil is uncertain, but to give it lasting peace lies with our nations, but to you they will be more grateful. If you decide for peace and alliance, you may assure to yourselves the lasting friendship of the Spartans freely offered by them, you on your part employing no force, but kindness only. All further competition between our states will be for the betterment of the people and shall be in the realms of science, art and material prosperity. Consider the great

advantages that such a friendship
will yield. If you and we are at
one for peace, you may be certain
that the rest of Hellas, which is
less powerful than we, will pay to
both of us the greatest deference
and we shall be impregnable against
the onslaught of any barbarian.

JASON

These are wise words and words that
should be the bases of all future
peace between men. They are a monument to a great people, and more
so since the Spartans are noted for
the brevity of their speech.

KING

As you say, it is our custom not to
say much where few words will suffice,
but on the contrary, we are most
liberal of speech when some weighty
communication has to be made and
words are the minister of action.

JASON

May I follow such wise words with
some of my own paltry ideas as to
the cause of the sickness that has
befallen our peoples.

KING

By all means. I don't know if
the cause can be known, but we must
in any case treat the sickness like
we are wise doctors who likewise not
knowing the cause of a sickness,
pretend to wisely treat it anyway.

JASON

Your allies fearing the wealth and
prosperity and growing power of Athens
resolved to form an alliance strong
enough to destroy us. Not feeling
strong enough themselves, they, thus,
came to you urging that you had a fear
of us for the same reason as they.
They deceived you in reality
into thinking you had something to
fear from our power, which is no more
than equal to your own wealth and
power. You fell into the trap of
such unwarranted fear because of
your natural sympathy for the more
impoverished of the earth. Your
practice of state ownership of
property that ensures moderate
prosperity for all citizens makes
you have a natural disposition
against the immoderate wealth of
many Athenians. You therefore
joined the impoverished nations,
where a few were rich and the rest
poor, out of principle and not out
of greed. You sincerely believe
our prosperity is derived from ex-
ploiting our neighbors and is a danger to your economic principles.
Thus you, as a matter of principle,
and not out of greed have opposed
us at any point of our weakness.
You believe in moderating greed;
we believe it is the very essence
of life. Thus we are faced with
the fact of two apparently non-re-
concilable ideals. As in any great
debate, there must be some truth
and some right on both sides of
the argument. We can best help

the cause of peace here, by discov-
ering the good in our respective
ideals and reconciling good with
good, these being compatible, we
must prove that peace is not only
possible, but profitable.

KING
Well spoken great captain of the
Athenians. Profit is one thing
that can be understood by either
private or public owners.

JASON
Now, we must discuss our differences.

KING
Our chief objection to Athenian influence is that people in the lands
of your control are forced into
poverty.

JASON
We object to the tyranny over men's
minds that is your way.

KING
We are opposed to the slavery impos-
ed on your neighbors by high taxes
and low wages.

JASON
You attempt to undermine our influence and cause mankind to hate us.

KING
You attack and overthrow governments
not friendly to your practices.

JASON
You do the same.

KING
(Getting angry) You, you, you, Athenians are a pack of liars and assassins.

JASON
And you are the chief assassin of the world.

KING
You are the chief back stabber and back biter from that loathsome city of back riders.

They have completely lost their cool, draw daggers, and try to stab each other, old men though they are.

JASON
Villain!

KING
Scoundrel!

JASON
Puppet!

KING
Greedy knave.

JASON
Tyrant!

KING
Mother of tyrants.

JASON
King of tyrants.

Suddenly as they started, they just stop and stare at each other in disbelief at what is happening.

>   JASON
> Are we peacemakers or foolish little
> boys arguing over whose father is
> the strongest?
>
>   KING
> I have no gift for name calling or
> I would really put the fire to your
> feet like when we were ten and you
> were sleeping on my father's throne.
>
>   JASON
> (Beginning to laugh) I too had more
> grievances in fancy than I seem to
> have in the real world. Grave as
> our differences are, we are great
> fools to be standing here shouting
> at each other. (They are both laugh-
> ing again and put up their daggers)
> What are we going to do to resolve
> our differences? Frankly, I don't
> have a clue. Our ideas of govern-
> ment are based on such ludicrously
> opposite extremes, it leads one to
> wonder if we haven't been chosen by
> the gods to be an entertainment ex-
> posing at once all of man's folly?
>
>   KING
> I too am similarly clueless. Perhaps
> we should declare peace is won and
> worry about the problems later.
>
>   JASON
> But that is why peace never lasts.

KING
All right. Adopt our system of
state ownership and give up your
greedy speculators to be fed to the
predators in our animal park.

JASON
What an absurd idea. Why don't you
put your bureaucrats in the lion's
den. They make everyone's life
miserable. Ask your people.

KING
Here we go again. Why don't we cut
one another's throats and let our
children worry about the problem?

JASON
Why not declare communal ownership
to be an equal partner of private
ownership. And members of communal
businesses will own shares.

KING
Good idea! Yes communes that
provide jobs and anyone can join
by buying shares.

JASON
We'll have the best of both worlds.
Let us make our proclamation. There
is no time to waste.

KING
I wonder why nobody has thought of
this before?

JASON
Yes. I too wonder?

CURTAINS
ACT III, SCENE I

ACT III, SCENE II

This scene takes place in Athens at the Agora. The peace meeting has taken place and a peace proposal is to be read publicly so that it can be debated by all citizens in preparations for a vote as to whether to ratify it. DIANA reads the proclamation. Many citizens are present. Greek democracy is defined in the hope that a better understanding of it will bring about peace between Athens and Sparta.

                    DIANA
(Disguised as a boy, she reads the peace proposal)
The King of Sparta and the Archon of Athens declare that the hostilities between the great cities of Athens and Sparta that have been raging for seven years is to be ended upon ratification by the respective governments of the following terms. These terms of peace and friendship have been arrived at without either party admitting to defeat or compulsion by the other side.

    1. Both sides agree to return all prisoners of war, property or other valuables captured during the course of the conflict.

    2. Both sides agree to abide by the laws of the other side.

    3. Communal property and private property will both be legal.

    4. Peace, freedom, and friend-

ship will be eternal between the parties based on a democratic form of government for all Greeks.

5. Democracy is defined as a system of government that guarantees that each male citizen will have one vote and one job. No man can be free unless he has an equal say in his government and a job to ward off poverty.

And may I add that you better take advantage of this offer while you have the chance, because there will never be another chance for real democracy even in the lifetime of the eternal gods.

ZEUS goes totally ballistic and hurls thunderbolts that obliterate the stage

                          BARRY
(Hiding under a table) This is the most outrageous crap I have ever heard.

                        STOOLITES
(With Barry) ZEUS is furious. If thunderbolts were crap, I'd be the richest man in Athens.

                        ORACALLIS
ZEUS does not like real democracy.

DIANA is torn and tattered and her burnt toga is still smoking from ZEUS' thunderbolts.

                    ORACALLIS (Conti.)
And woe to those who know the future and warn men of its dangers.

A bolt strikes DIANA in the butt and she hotfoots off holding her butt. She stops short of the exit and shakes her fist toward heaven.

> DIANA
> I am not sorry, you big bully.

DIANA exists hastily as more thunderbolts crash down in her direction.

> SOCRATES
> Methinks it has been a bad day for bully gods, sophists and chatty goddesses.

> DIODOTUS
> Why SOCRATES? There still has to be a vote. We may not have peace or democracy if the tyrants have their way.

> SOCRATES
> Tyrants days are numbered. Truth has been spoken by men and gods for the first time in history and truth is more important than any vote. Votes can always be reversed, but when once truth sees the light of day no darkness can hide it?

> ARISTOPHENES
> You mean that the lexicographers and politicians have been bullying us all along with bad definitions? No wonder we are all in the political dark.

> SOCRATES
> You gather my meaning correctly, ARISTOPHENES. In a word, we have been worded by the demagogues into believing in words that have worded words

into meaningless sophistry.

DIODOTUS
Your meaning is murky SOCRATES. Is democracy such a mushy term?

SOCRATES
A feast of mush for rabble-rousers. It has a different meaning for every man. Is there any wonder the demagogues are such clever political jugglers?

HERCULES
Democracy has nothing to do with jobs. I will not hire every fool who wants a job. I would soon go broke.

SOCRATES
Then you are not a democrat. There can be no democracy until every man is employed who wants a job.

BARRY
And where will this insanity end? Will children, slaves and women have jobs too?

GENERAL
If we must obey their laws, our hills will be covered with dying infants parents claim are not fit to live because no one will hire them.

BARRY
He is right. The Athenians are extreme in all things. They will use this law to shirk their responsibility to replenish us with citizens.

GENERAL
And I will not be able to defend
the city without many citizens ready
to die in defense of our walls.

ARISTOPHENES
You have about as much faith in your
fellow citizens as I have in your
generalship, which is none.

HERCULES
And what good can come of this common ownership? Soon after this is
allowed they will want my money.

BARRY
Greed and sharing are strange bedfellows. Too strange for me.

SOCRATES
Some men wish to work for the common good and some men against.
Both have a right to exist without
fear of the other.

BARRY
We shall see. I will speak against
all such dangerous innovation when
the assembly meets in three days.
I say death to Spartans and death
to their ideas. (Cheering)

DIODOTUS
And I will speak for innovation and
peace.

BARRY
(Aside to his followers) You must
get all our followers up early and
fill the amphitheater. Only those

seated get to vote. In three days,
we will have war.

DIODOTUS
(Aside to his followers) You must
all get up early. Peace or war
hinges on who gets up the earliest
and finds a seat in the amphitheater.

ARISTOPHENES
Future world history depends entirely
on which early bird gets the vote.

SOCRATES
Reason is helpless against the sleeping habits of hawks and doves.

CURTAINS
ACT III, SCENE II

ACT III, SCENE III

The women of Athens and Sparta hold a secret meeting at the temple of DIANA. They are determined that peace shall succeed, and accordingly make various plans to make sure the men vote in favor of it. There are about ten women who show up to represent the other women. DIANA; QUEEN KRUSHAMEMNON; LYSISTRATA, SR; and LYSISTRATA, JR do most of the talking. DIANA is talking to the eye of ZEUS TV camera at the rise.

DIANA
This is your eye of ZEUS TV reporter
coming to you from my own temple
where the women of Athens and Sparta
are meeting to discuss the forthcoming votes on peace by their men. I
will do all in my power to dissuade
these women from any illegal
interference in the wise deliberations

of their men, as they have no legal rights
as citizens. I also wish to lodge a
protest about the nerve these women
have meeting at my house. Apollo is
hiding inside waiting impatiently to
have our daily joint prayer session.
ZEUS has every right to be angry with
these foolish women who are interfer-
ing in his supplicant's ablutions. We
always take a hot bath before praying.
Here they come.

The women file in and stop in front of the temple where they will hold their meeting. QUEEN KRUSHAMEMNON is the first to speak.

              QUEEN
Women of Athens and Sparta. We are
gathered here to make sure our men
end this senseless and stupid war.
Are there any suggestions about how
we can make sure they vote for peace?

              DIANA
(In full haughty goddess accoutrement)
I must warn you that the gods are
against this illegal interference in
the affairs of the men. You have no legal
rights and never will

The women who have come with pots and pans and vegetables and fruits and other feminine accoutrement trash DIANA in front of her temple chasing her away.

              QUEEN
If there are any other spies or turn-
coats present, they better speak up
now or face an even worse wrath.

              MRS. JASON
If there are, they will feel the blade

of my rolling pin.

The women all cheer MRS. JASON.

>QUEEN
>The women of Sparta have decided we
>will go on strike against our men.
>We will deny them breakfast, darning
>of their socks, sewing on buttons
>and other conjugal pleasures less
>important.

>MRS. JASON
>I will not be so respectful of the
>gods as I hitherto have been. I will
>let them keep their vintage wines
>and fine jewelry they ply me with in
>return for my favors. The men of
>Athens will then have to fear the
>wrath of the gods until they stop
>this foolish war.

>LYSISTRATA
>I don't think you should make such a
>great sacrifice MAMMA. And DADDY
>would be much humiliated if you came
>out of the closet and admitted such
>infidelities, even with gods who are
>well known to be scoundrels.

>MRS. JASON
>Just because I was fooled by one pop-
>injay doesn't mean all of my sacrifices
>have been in vain.

>LYSISTRATA
>Yes mother. But I have a safer
>plan for the women of Athens. Women,
>why don't we disguise ourselves as

men, get up earlier than they do
and take all the places in the
amphitheatre? That way we can vote
for peace ourselves and not depend
on the perfidy of witless men.

          MRS. JASON,
Yes. We did that once before and it
worked. We voted in communal sharing
of everything including sex, but the
men got onto us and voted it out after
a year's trial. They didn't want to share
pots, pans or old hags. Men are selfish
and stupid.

          LYSISTRATA
Then what have we got to lose by
trying that tactic again. What
say you sisters. Are you for fool-
ing the men again?

The women all favor this course of action.

          LYSISTRATA
Than it is all agreed. We will disguise ourselves as men and vote for
peace.

MARCHELLO MACHIAVELLI comes out of hiding.

          MACHIAVELLI
(Dressed as Apollo) Wait women of
Greece. You must re-consider. Gods
and men need war. Where else will
you get slaves and gold and jewels and
other loot? And we need bribes even
more than deceiving sophist orators

          DIANA
(Joins Apollo) I agree with dressing

like men, but peace is hated by the gods.
War is true wisdom. How else would
men have the chance to bribe us to save
their pitiful lives? And it gives us a chance
to show off our mercifulness, one of my
favorite chores. I once rescued this
beautiful maiden about to be ravished by
ZEUS. (ZEUS thunders) Not fast enough
to ruin the entertainment of course. I must
admit I have a soft spot for hairy half horse
half men gods in disguise who
are much too good for mere mortals.
(ZEUS is much annoyed again)

                    LYSISTRATA
            Doesn't that Apollo look a lot like
            the Roman ambassador MAMMA?

                    MRS. JASON
            It is indeed that same cheapskate.

DIANA is furious to learn that Apollo is the Roman ambassador.

                    DIANA
            I thought you were less than a god
            you Roman imposter. And I agree with
            these women. Men should be punished
            for making war instead of love.

All the women attack Apollo leaving him in tatters, if not completely nude, bruised and bleeding.

                    QUEEN KRUSH.
            Enough punishment women of Greece.
            If we are to make peace between
            Sparta and Athens, we must not start
            by making war on men. There are
            better uses for them. Even this
            Roman dog that I also recognize as
            the Roman spy who came to my house.

Let us go back to our houses and
put our plans into action.

The women file out leaving the bruised and battered MACHIAVELLI to be helped into the temple by DIANA who has had a change of heart.

DIANA
Come Roman pony. You'll do until I
find a real stallion.

**CURTAINS
ACT III, SCENE III**

ACT IV, SCENE I

This scene takes place at the Amphitheater where the Athenian assembly meets to make laws. The rule is that any Athenian male citizen who gets up early enough to get to the Amphitheater and take a seat gets to vote on the laws that day. Many people are turned away on this important day when Athens is to vote for war or peace with Sparta. STOOLITES is in charge of checking for proper citizenship and finds that many of those favoring peace have some reason to be disqualified such as women disguised as men. MACHIAVELLI has warned the hawks of this trick. DIANA and LYSISTRATA in disguise wearing fake beards or mustaches to hide their identity are turned down and get mean.

LYSISTRATA
Let us pass collector of dung before
we throw some in your face.

DIANA
Out of my way mortal before I turn
you into a dung beetle for real.

STOOLITES
Everyone is to be checked to see
that they are of the male gender.
Let me pull your beards and look

under those togas.

STOOLITES attempts to pull beards and grab togas but is roundly caned with the staffs they carry. They run off just as HERCULES shows up in time to help STOOLITES.

                    HERCULES
Those two hooligans were killing you.
Why didn't you let them pass?

                    STOOLITES
We got a tip from the Roman ambassador to be on the lookout for women
disguised as men. They planned to
vote for peace and ruin us all.

                    HERCULES
Good work STOOLITES. But what of
the rest of DIODOTUS' followers? He
has all the many followers of SOCRATES,
who do more foolish talking than acting
and besides those all the degenerates who like
comedy. They are many, but an undis-
ciplined rabble.

                    STOOLITES
The Amphitheater is packed with our
followers. I accused many of
DIODOTUS' followers of being women
in disguise and I think many of them
were, because they left without much
argument after I tried to look under
their togas.

                    HERCULES
Brilliant! But some tried to get by
you?

                    STOOLITES
One claimed to have lost his genitals

                    to a Spartan sword and showed me the
                    scars from his wound. I could not
                    really tell the difference, but I
                    let him be seated when he said he
                    was against infanticide.

                              HERCULES
                    Even if it was a trick about the genitals
                    pro lifers of a certainty are of our party.
                    But wait, here comes that trouble
                    maker SOCRATES leaning on two boys.

The two boys are two women who are determined to vote for peace.

                              STOOLITES
                    I'll get rid of him, just see. Sir,
                    sir is that not a false beard you
                    wear? I suspect you of being a
                    woman and women cannot vote. And
                    those two lads you cavort with, I
                    am certain they are lads you have
                    corrupted, but I still must have a
                    look at their equipage to be sure
                    of their gender.

STOOLITES reaches toward SOCRATES' beard and is grabbed by the balls by SOCRATES.
                              SOCRATES
                    You dare keep the women from voting
                    dung beetle? The last time they
                    snuck in here and voted, they voted
                    in free love and I got laid more that
                    year than in my whole life put to-
                    gether.

SOCRATES drops STOOLITES howling in pain and he and the two ladies who caned Hercules the while enter the amphitheater and take seats. Curithias, Aristophenes and others are already seated. JASON is officiating and is ready to start the proceedings.

JASON
Under our duty as Archon of the
Athenian people we declare this
legislative body to be open. Today
we must decide on the issue of
war or peace with Sparta. There is
a peace agreement that has been
drawn up by the two principal warring
cities, that if ratified by this body
and the Spartan nobles, will become the
basis for a lasting peace between the
two cities. We believe it is in the
best interest of Athens to ratify
this document and we back it with all
our prestige, but it is up to you,
the citizens of this democracy to
make the final decision. Are there
any requests to speak before we vote?

No one makes a direct request, but soon there begins, one at a time, a chant of "BARRY" which grows to a multitude. BARRY, as though surprised and reluctant, agrees to speak.

BARRY
I will speak, but not happily.

JASON
BARRY PANASSES will bray... whoops...
I mean speak.

BARRY takes JASON'S place on the hustings (Bema). Long pause as though gathering his well-prepared thoughts.

BARRY
I with great reluctance and some
amount of chastisement once again
agree to be councilor to the Athenians. I must say that I have been sorely
intimidated by the false charges of
intimidation laid upon my assertions

about false patriots during my last
speech. (Laughs) I, however, in spite
of the rejection of my proposals for
your welfare at our last assembly, do
not come back to you a bitter and
hardened loser. My wits, I must admit, are considerably dulled, because
of the considerable amount of sleep
I have lost thinking of the lasting
damage that has been done to your
future by my well-meaning adversary.
To try, therefore, to avoid being
unfairly accused of casting aspersions
on my well meaning if somewhat biased
adversary, (Laughs) I will confine
these remarks to things revealed to
me in dreams that came to me in the
small snatches of sleep I got amid my
ponderings over the fate of our ill-
lustrious city. I must warn you, however,
my well-meaning foe will in all likelihood
find some well-meaning way to question
the honesty of my dreams. This being a
democracy, I am the first
to acquiesce to the superior wisdom
of the vote. It proves that wisdom
is power and that might is right.
I stand firmly convinced then, that
peace is the proper position for our
city, because your power has convinced me. It has also convinced me
that power and might being the end
of all good, for what is more good
than the power of the state, that
Athens should always be as powerful
as possible when dealing with her
enemies. Some among us will probably
find a way to pervert this concept
to their own ends, but men of cowardice are the most resourceful of men.

Consider my dream: we are negotiating
with our most formidable enemy. One
that for seven years has tried in
every way to destroy us. They claim
their willingness to negotiate is
from a position of insolence and power and that peace, now mark this,
while not, not I say, expeditious,
as claimed by one of our well meaning
orators, is humanitarian after seven
long years of bloody warfare. I
awaked from this dream relieved that
I was dreaming, only to find out I
was not dreaming. In short, I waked
to find out that these insolent rascals not only wish to steal our first
great land and sea victory over them,
but we must reward their generosity
by returning their spent ships and
men and all their captured cities as
a sign that we regret their imminent
destruction. I may now once again
be dreaming, but I for one would re-
joice to see them all who have slaugh-
tered ours sons and fathers for the
last seven years destroyed to the
last man. (Delirious cheering. BARRY
knows he has them.)
We Athenians, reputed to be the wisest
of mortals, would let the Spartans,
reputed to be the dullest of mortals,
pull the wool over our eyes in such
an easy fashion. The fact that we
are in a position to destroy their
power once and for all is of no sig-
nificance. Our cowardly leaders are
afraid to fight so we must listen to
such insolence when we are on the
brink of victory. If this is the
obsequity we have come to, I agree

that peace is a wise cause. Yet to
make peace and refund to them their
power to break another alliance and
destroy us, is more than I can swal-
low, even if I am dreaming. We must
remove their capacity to make war or
this peace is utter foolishness that
will be a disservice to both cities.
We have their army trapped and their
fleet is in our hands. Let us as
our peace making right, since it is
in our power and we have the might,
assure peace by destroying these
instruments of war and the men who
wield them. When you destroy the
Spartan war machine, you will do no
more than when you destroyed my hopes
for Athenian supremacy by expressing
your wish for an end to this just
war that is tantamount to surrender-
ing to the enemy. If you do as I
suggest is just, they must, as I
have done, then accept peace on your
terms. Then, you will be master of
Hellas and peace will be permanent.
Failing in this course, the future
of Athens does not exist and I will
be the first to open my veins and
let flow the river of blood that
will be our future.

Cheers and a chant for war follow BARRY'S speech until GENERAL AGAMEMNON'S request to speak is granted. He takes his place on the hustings and makes a report on the battlefield situation, which is less than cheerful. He shocks everyone by recommending peace.

> GENERAL
> I too am in favor of destroying the
> Spartan war machine, but less you
> become victimized by overconfidence

the main nemesis of all victories, I feel it is my duty to correctly assess the prospects of victory. I have none of the tricks of the speech making art that often rules your lives so I will confine myself to giving you only the facts. It is true that we have captured the enemies fleet which by agreement of this proposed peace treaty, we must return if peace is declared. But the final victory cannot be won at sea. The timbers of these ships are not the walls and will of Sparta. It is true that we have a Spartan led army trapped on an island where they cannot escape; yet the number of Spartans is insignificant. More die each year falling down wells than would be destroyed on this island. Most of those trapped are allies of Sparta, who are not at the heart of Spartan power. Our risk in attempting to destroy these however is great. They are well provisioned and fortified. We may not be able to defeat them and a long siege is impossible as we could not supply a large army in winter. Thus, we could become the trapped and victory would be snatched by defeat. Our whole army might then be destroyed by our own folly. We generals are not men of the people who let their emotions gain the better of their senses; we are men of reality. The risk of this venture is great and the gain is small. We who were the first to recommend war when the conditions were more favorable, in good

conscience cannot now but recommend
peace to the Athenian people.

At the end of this speech, all pandemonium breaks out. There are now many boos mixed with chants of war. BARRY, who at first is as shocked as everyone else at this defection of his staunch ally, finally breaks the impasse by speaking out.

          BARRY
(From the crowd) My dear old friend
GENERAL ULYSESUS S. AGAMEMNON,
when have generals learned so much con-
templation? Was it not the advice
of the greatest Athenian general
Demosthenes, to his soldiers to fight
and not to think, as thinking brings
fear and weakness and cowardice? Is
not thought, fear of action? Are
you not the leading coward of the
country since you are supposed to
fight and in reality you spend your
days thinking about defeat?

          GENERAL
If you are so brave and I am such
a coward, I will here and now resign
my command to you and you can lead
the Athenian forces too glorious
victory.

          BARRY
You are a common coward, afraid to
fight and should share the fate of
your more noble predecessors.

          GENERAL
Athenians who gave me this command,
if it is the will of this assembly,
I will fall on my sword and turn
over my command of the Athenian

forces to MAD CAL PANASSES and
may the gods favor your enterprise.

ASSEMBLY
(Roaring approval) Hail GENERAL PAN-
ASSES.

The general falls on his sword.

BARRY
Wait GENERAL! Wait! Wait! Let us
not be hasty. I am not a soldier.

ASSEMBLY
(Approval of crowd) Hail GENERAL
PANASSES. Long live GENERAL PAN-
ASSES! Long live Athens!

BARRY
Stop! Stop! I have no experience.
I am a sophist, a rhetorician, a
paid orator. Would you entrust the
future of your city to a demagogue?

HERCULES
Bravery is worth more than any experience.

ORACALLIS
The gods give victory to the brave.

STOOLITES
Crappots forever.

BARRY
No, no, no. I resign this commis-
sion... I am not worthy.

DIODOTUS
(To the bema) Hear me o great multi-

tude. Give me your ears. Hear me!
I have opposed BARRY in the past
and I still oppose his policies.
However, I am now in full agreement
with him that our fate cannot be put
into such incompetent hands. Victories are not won by bravery alone.
Otherwise there would never be a
loser. Victories are won by the wise
who know how to wait for the wisest
moment to strike the enemy at his
weakest point. Do not be misled by
the gods. They care little for the
brave and would just as soon the worst
coward in the world won this war.
BARRY does not feign cowardice to find
favor with the gods or avoid the toil
of war. Fear has made him prudent
and wise. He knows his folly will
lead to disaster.

              HERCULES
Down with DIODOTUS. We want peace.
Destroy the Spartans. We want peace!

DIODOTUS is booed and is drowned out by chants of BARRY.

                BARRY
Let the soothsayer decide. (Throws
ORACALLIS a bag of money) What say
you ORACALLIS? And I want an ob-
jective opinion.

              ORACALLIS
There will be peace if BARRY leads
the Athenian forces to victory.
The leading gods favor peace.
(A roll of thunder) You see Athenians.
ZEUS puts his stamp of approval
on my predictions.

DIODOTUS
No. Don't listen to him. He has
been bribed.

BARRY
The gods have spoken. I must obey
the gods and lead the Athenian people
to victory.

DIODOTUS
Hear me, hear me! This is Mad Cal
madness.

BARRY
I am to be the savior of Athens. We
will at long last have peace. Down
with DIODOTUS. Ostracize him.

There is a great tumult of shouting to ostracize DIODOTUS. DIODOTUS attempts to speak but is shouted down. JASON takes the gavel and calls for order.

JASON
Order, order. This is still a democracy. We have a request to speak.
DIODOTUS will speak.

DIODOTUS
This may well be my last counsel to
you my fellow citizens of Athens.
Up until this day, however heinous
some men have held us up to be,
there has been a certain admiration
for the boldness and humanity with
which we have dispatched sorted conventional
values in favor of that which has grace
and style and wit. Today however you
have made the grave error of dispatching wit in favor of the half
wit, and even victory will be de-

feat, because you will everyday app-
roach the inevitable doom of those
who earn the hatred of mankind. A
policy of witless hatred, greed and
war can only lead in the end to
the witless destruction of all that is
precious to both sides. To destroy an
enemy at all cost is mad indeed. Peace
is peace, democracy is democracy,
freedom is freedom, but war is death.
Freedom is not slavery to greed,
democracy is not a republic of fools,
and peace is not war as BARRY would
have you believe. Neither side in
this internecine struggle is strong
enough to survive an all out war. Only
the mutual enemies of Greece will benefit.
If you choose to follow a demagogue like
BARRY down the road of injustice and
inhumanity and unregenerate greed,
I freely choose ostrasization. If
BARRY assumes the generalship of our
glorious city I will accept your
verdict of ostracization from Athens
and however sadly seek a new home in
some strange land where hope may
still exist; for your fate will be
sealed forever. I ask your verdict?

There is an overwhelming chant of "ostracize" etc. and then, "long live GENERAL PANASSES". DIODOTUS leaves the bema-speaking platform with head held high and BARRY takes his place.

BARRY
Thank you my fellow citizens. I
only have one request. Temporary
martial law. Temporary dictatorial
powers.

ASSEMBLY

Dictator, dictator etc.

CURTAINS
ACT IV, SCENE I

ACT IV, SCENE II

She is having her long hair done by a slave.

APHRODISI
Careful LILA dear that not a hair
is out of place or I shall see that
you are married to a satyr and made
to raise a family of goats.

LILA
A satyr is better than a man anytime.

APHRO
This was a careless threat that offered more reward than punishment.
I shall give you an astronomer who
is always looking at the stars.

LILA
Then I shall raise a brood of stars
who will be as eternal as the night.

APHRO
I can see that a man in any form is
not a worthy punishment. I am expecting a romantic myself; so hurry
your job to completion and you can
go for a ride on his valet. My lover
gallops like a Roman racehorse, but
his valet looks like a real Italian
stallion.

LILA

Are the Romans from Nubia?

APHRO.
To hear them talk you would think
so, but they'll do in a pinch.

MACHIAVELLI enters with his valet, A STALLONE look-a-like if possible. The slave carries food and wine. He and LILA take off for LILA'S bedroom.

MARCHELLO
(Ebullient) Anybody home?

APHRO.
I haven't been allowed to leave here
in years you boob. What offerings
have you brought Apollo? Gods do
not live by promises alone.

MARCHELLO
All the delicacies of Rome. Bread,
cheese and tomato paste, wine,
candles for the virgins...

APHRO
What is so special about bread,
cheese and tomato paste.

MARCHELLO
You haven't lived until you've had
Roman pizza.

APHRO.
Anyway we can always use candles.
They disappear fast around here with
100 virgins making daily sacrifices
to Apollo. I'm sure that attractive
young valet of yours will help light
the candles while he's here.

MAC
I'm thinking of donating him to
Apollo for your choir. After he is
a made eunuch of course. They sing
so well

SYLVESTOR
But boss, I'm already a made man.

LILA
The choir is all Greek volunteers
sir.

MARCHELLO
You're going to have a hellava time
here Sylvestor.

APHRO
You may go LILA. And take this insolent slave with you. See that his
instrument is well tuned. I might
want to hear him sing sometime. And
I don't mean soprano. And see to it
that my prayers are not disturbed.

LILA
Yes mistress. (They exit hand in hand.
He carries a panpipe)

APHRO.
I hear there is much for Rome to
celebrate. The Athenians have attacked the trapped Spartan army
while declaring themselves for peace.
Is there some great mix-up?

MAC.
They have begun a new fashion. They
have re-named war and call it peace.
The Spartans are very angry and vow

to never discuss anything with the
Athenians again.

APHRO.
Greek enemies are feeling good today.
No wonder you brought so much wine.

MAC.
I admit, Rome is feeling a bit expansive and I shall be promoted by the senate. We shall eat drink and make love to celebrate Athenian victory.

APHRO.
You mean your victory. The chance of peace in Hellas has been lost forever.

MAC.
(Taking her in his arms) It is also your victory. Don't forget you promised each side that god was on their side. And like dummies they both pledged you plunder if they won. You'll be rich. I mean Apollo will be rich.

APHRO.
This is true. War is not so bad if there is good plunder. JASON gave his word. Where is he? Does he lead the attack on Sphagiea?

MAC.
APOLLO forbid. The Archon's job is only ceremonial. His main job is to see to it that the gods are kept happy. That is why he promised you so much plunder. He promised the

same to many other gods. Common
soldiers will steal most of it.

APHRO.
That dirty welcher. I will pray
for war until every dirty devious
Greek is dead.

MAC.
(Aside) What a diplomat I am. (Back
to Aphro.) Don't worry. There's
going to be enough loot to go around.
They'll give you some loot to play
it safe. Men are craven cowards
where it concerns the gods.

APHRO.
If JASON is not leading the attack,
who is?

MAC.
The greatest coward in the world.
The demagogue known as MAD CAL
PANASSES.

APHRO.
Impossible. He is a certifiable fool.

MAC.
Never the less, the Athenians are
victorious. They have destroyed the
Spartan army on Sphagiae and are putting the whole population to the sword.

APHRO.
Done like a true coward. But stop
being like Tantalus. Give me the
whole unabridged tale.

MAC.
The valiant men who were defending

the island were frightened out of
their wits by the barbarous screams
of BARRY and his friends. They
thought they were being attacked
by a mighty army of men from hell,
but in reality it was screams of pure
terror, because BARRY'S cowards were
forced to fight against their will.
The Spartans were quite fooled by
this tactic. It is rumored that the
Simple-minded loafer SOCRATES
who is always asking endless questions
suggested this tactic. Next and
what would be logical for an army
of cowards, they put their slaves in
the front line only equipped with
dirt and pepper. Curithias, the
spice merchant, supplied and trained
this army of slaves. When the Spartans who are not too swift finally
figured out that they were being
attacked by an army of cowards,
they attacked with great ferocity
only to be sprayed in the eyes
with pepper. This tactic completely
disconcerted the Spartans who by
now were deafened and blinded and
soon beheaded. BARRY is a great
hero for thinking of this tactic and
has been elected dictator of Athens
for life. He has declared peace
eternal with the Spartans and after
Curithias became the only Athenian
fatality of the attack, he made
pepper a PANASSES family monopoly.
A marble statue of Curithias has
been commissioned and he has been
declared a god. Funding of this statue
must come from temple loot, since it is
to the gods benefit.

APHRO.
Over my dead body it will. This just proves one thing though. There is a thin line between genius and imbecility. I wonder why no one thought of this pepper weapon before. It seems so obvious it's stupid.

MAC.
It won't last though. It seems the cooks hate the idea and threaten to go on strike if there is a shortage of pepper. Without cooks, men would have to give up war.

APHRO.
It is an age of madness when mere eloquent liars and exaggerators become leaders of great nations.

MAC.
Let us stop all this thinking and start the war of love.

APHRO
Get out!

MAC.
What's wrong? We have much to celebrate.

APHRO.
Get out! You have tricked me. Demagogues in the pay of Roman spies have tricked Greece. I see now that there is no profit to be made out of war. Greece is finished and so am I.

MAC.
(Exits laughing) Ave atque vale particeps crininis. (Hail and farewell my accomplice)

CURTAINS
ACT IV, SCENE II

ACT IV, SCENE III

BARRY makes his way over a battlefield littered with the debris of battle, bloody sword in hand, stabbing and killing the wounded and helpless, gloating madly over his victory. From time to time a former friend, foe or god in ghostly visage appears and frightens him out of his wits when he hacks at them with no apparent effect. There is no effect because they are ghosts. ORACALLIS is the first figment of BARRY'S bad conscience to appear.

ORACALLIS
Oh great DIONYSIS, your feckless son the world doth rule.
Mighty victory has his madness won, while his enemies to the underworld run.
As wine is blood, much your cup doth runneth over.
Thy libation bearing son, great harvest flesh doth reap.
Now all women and children of Hellas to your alter shall come and weep.
Rich shall be thy plunder as mighty ZEUS does thunder.
Oh great god of the passions, as wine doth obscure the conscience from man, you shall hide the world from your votaries.
Lovers of thy great priest, MAD CAL BARRY, think you grateful oneness, who the world doth make merry.
By men's blood you live, as they mind not giving, for man is but a

vine his life a grape to crush.
Man, who by frolic acts the fool,
and boisterously your philosophy
would embrace, shall wither in a day,
and fall the god of passion's play.
Who among you would to the heavens
fly in bloody revery, follow then
the feckless BARRY.
He knows the tricky path through
the underbrush above.
And I think you will agree, his
ideas were born in the other world
below, and have the fetid odor of
the tyrants cloven toe.

          BARRY
I heard that fetid speech. (Hacks
at him in vain) Die traitor die.
What ho. Is it a shade of my over-
heated imagination? Another!

         APHRODISI
Beauty's cup is by the ass drained
dry. Oh gods, come no more to this
once fair land, for all that was
is soon this molested earth to stain.
And all art and science, food for
the immortal worm.
No more the flesh of women shall
caress your wanton worshippers.
Down, down, down to the shades of hell,
will all descend alike.
For mind banished from this sacred
soil, takes with it the best hope of
man. The gods pity this man BARRY,
for he does their work too well, and
will in all likelihood, become the
king of hell.
Long live BARRY, king of hell!

BARRY
(Hacking futilely) Die you priestess
from hell and die all you foes of
freedom. Go to the shades where
you belong. Join alliance with Cer-
berus, for dog should watch dog.
Go to dark death, you dark Spartans.
The soil of Hellas shall no longer
by dull sharing grimfaces be spoiled.
Afore today, you were the mighty. Ha!
Where are you now, you flighty shades?
Oh men, who would put the lie to BARRY,
you as your rich reward, sup on the
tasty sword. Come forth! Come to
its sharp caresses. Hellas would be
purified. A million times a million
die to purge the race, a small sacrifice to please the gods. One night
of hell raising in Hellas will overcome the loss. No more the cowards
live and love under marble hill.
Better far, their graves they fill.
Employment have I found in this
friendly sword. Like a kind of
gruesome Cupid, I match life with
death; to kill, that is the message.
The meaning of this sharp point?
To slaughter men of course. What
after all is man, but fresh meat;
in time of peace, he fattens and
gets ready for the kill. Life has
no deeper meaning; of this gory
thought, man must drink his fill.

LYSISTRATA
The love of maidens doth strew this
hill. Soon too, my life shall drain
and flow away. Oh great gods of
heaven, what kind of cads are thee,

to drink so mercilessly? Oh life,
my impure thoughts do best me. I
cannot hold them back. The dam has
broke and evil fills my soul, where
once was naught but vagrant virginity.
Oh, my great and beautiful love, I
cannot bear these thoughts and worse.
We die when only born a week. What
means a world that destroys such love
as ours?

ATLAS
We are out of step with the change
in times. Beloved Hellas died today. When great nations die, it
is the death of life as well. Sweet
freedom, art and love doth leave
this land today. We seeds of freedom's thought shall do the same.
To live and give birth to immortal
minds.

LYSISTRATA
Oh great love of mine, all is lost.
Let us to yonder chasm go, and
quickly, forsake this land of hate,
by jumping to our deaths, embracing
to the end. Nevermore to part, our
love living on in the world below.

ATLAS
To this destiny, we honor bound
would go, before we slaves would be.
But now there is a higher duty, a
living trust. There is a ship in
yonder bay, which to the new world
goes. Over unknown seas, we shall
sail, sacred duty bound. Hope's
green land is somewhere far away,
in that west, where there our race

must grow. We dared the gods, whose
destruction we do reap, yet now we
know for sure, a higher place we see.
This race that has dared to hope,
man's life is free, must not perish.
Let us go and love. Our loins will
overcome, the stench of stupidity.

LYSISTRATA
Women's wisdom does not always fit
her grace my love. Methinks your
plan will better serve the future
of our race. Go my love, that we
may live and love, even though it be,
on some unknown apogee. I come with
thee.

BARRY
(Hacking in vain) Deserters, fools
Spartans. I care not which. I shall
cleanse the race of the weak. More
Spartans. Bring more Spartans that I
may purge them of their fetid lives.

GENERAL AGAMEMNON
(Bloody sword in hand) Do you have
ample dirt to throw in their eyes?

BARRY
Has jealousy come to claim the victory? How many more victories Athens
would own, if you had a bag of tricks,
O GENERAL DULL.

GENERAL
Oh gods, protect glorious Athens from
fickle fortunes tawdry triumph.

BARRY
By this capture we drive them to

their walls. Sweet Athens! By my
monuments you shall be known. Dross-
full nations have none. Where are
your splendid monuments Sparta?
Even the bricks and stones of your
walls will soon be dust. Now that
it is my time, fair Athens, draw
your cloak about your pale shoulders,
mask thy mind to former friends.
No longer do we bare the breast for
free, for I shall set the fashion,
to wit, a pariah nation, BARRY'S own.
In knowledge, our great commodity,
charily will we give, most like a
women, guarding her coveted chastity.
Apostatizing from the human race,
we'll live within our walls, pretending that my cloak, enfolds the
heavens and the earth.

GENERAL
Methinks you have suffered a fast
case of megalomania my dear dictator.
In this, Athens has her fortune made.

BARRY
Out of my sight General Nuisance. But
here is an admirer.

HERCULES
Workers will be busy in the foundry.
Broken weapons pave this holy field,
like the early droppings of the fig
tree. No want of jobs, no hungry
mouths, no complaining louts do I
foresee, and astute investors happy
talents count. The richest nation
shall we be, if Hellas does not run
out of Greeks. Mother's many sons,
hurry you, come you to this world,

that glorious battle you may seek.
When winter falls and battles halt,
Much love you youths and maidens make.
Athens, by your warrior sons, in
death, like no nation in life, shall
prosper, for the god's good entertainment, directed by that fool BARRY.
Amazing how a little gold can make
a little god.

BARRY
That's an insult. I will take
all your gold soon and we shall see
who is the fool. But wait. Here
come some worthy Spartans for me
to kill.

GENERAL MALICIOUS GEORGIUSES and KING KRUSHAMEMNON are helping each other across the carnage and fall down exhausted. BARRY is kind of cowing back in fear of these two mighty Spartans.

GEORGI
What say you now oh great fool,
that I return from the underworld
to tell you I told you so.

KRUSH.
Your way would have ended the same.
I postponed the inevitable for a
time and that is something.

GEORGI
We could have struck first and the
cowards would have run away. Their
leader is no fool though. That
devious trick they pulled on us was
worthy of the heroes of Troy.

BARRY

These Spartans are not as bad as
I thought.

KRUSH.

A traditional Greek I must admit.
But then, opinion is easy after
the battle is lost. We will soon
turn this small loss to our great
advantage. Consider. Now our party
feels wronged by the deceit of the
Athenians. The next battle will be
for the honor of Hellas. If the
Athenians want peace, we shall show
them peace.

GENERAL M.

I go back to Hades to await the heroes
of your peace.

KRUSH.

Oh gods, the death of peace is sad to
see. Sparta could have thrived on
peace and led the world in green
olive trees. Now coiled hate will
live in perpetuity. We bleed ourselves of blood and wealth as though
this were the natural order of things.
Where can this lead to, but death of
Greek liberty? I did my part, I
tried in vain. Now beware! The great
king Xerxes, like fiery Apollo,
will come from the east, leaving
darkness in his wake. Wait for
me GENERAL HELLHOUND.

BARRY

The great paradox of life is that
prophets and murderers are never
respected in their own lands. But
wait. It is Apollo. He taught me

the art of genuflection you must know
to win favor of the gods.

           MACHIAVILLI
(Apollo impersonator) Oh great un-
forgiving gods of Hellas, your sons
you must love well, to take so many
to hell, known euphemistically as
the Elysium Fields, that blessed
place where heroes go, to rest peace-
fully in the arms of seven lustful
virgins. This is a great monument
here made of human bones and fetid
flesh, where once the power of the
world marched in step. Yea what a
marvelous mess, fit only for crows,
vermin and virgins. It is a good
days work BARRY. Where hopes of
Hellas die, the stock of Rome does
rise. Much cheer have I, to Tiber
town, the soon great Rome to tell.
What little Grecian cheer is left,
will soon be none. The demagogue
fool great Athens leads, who by the
sword would do well by all men.
Life leads to death by this futile
fratricide, for man is brother of
man. If I were not a Roman in disguise, I'd shed a tear in wonderment,
at such witty fools. Being a Roman,
I can only say, long live BARRY,
the DR. DEATH of Athens. As all
extremes are the road to death, on
BARRY'S beaten path, the Greeks shall
die, and Rome shall gain ascendancy

           BARRY
Vile Roman. I have been a fool, but
what is this? The vilest Athenian of
them all comes to scavenge for the

gods? Give them the fools gold old fool.

JASON

Men of Athens, you have destroyed
the world. All is gone. The tyranny
of passion has won the soul of our
fair state. A tragedy of errors
will rule the day. Ignorance and
madness have combined in licit intercourse. The soul of Athens has
aborted its future in a human garbage pale. I implore you O great
gods of Athens, before you deliver
us to our deserved destruction, give
us one more chance. We know not what
we do and know not who we are, thanks
to the fetid speech of the dastardly
demagogue BARRY. His speech, all full
of flowery flatteries and flaming
figments of partial truth, salted
and peppered with outright lies and
other exotic condiments dangerous
to the minds digestion, have over-
  whemed our democratic process, but
even though the path lead to hell,
we meant well. Give us therefore
one more chance, before you condem
us, O great ZEUS, that sober heads
may once again prevail. End this
damned bloody whore, this unholy war.

BARRY
He is totally mad.

ZEUS
(Entering deux ex machina) Mortal
man, I come to you to confide in
you my plan, the best kind I believe.
My plan for you is this. None what-
soever. I created you in a burst of

uninhibited creative foolery that I
often regret. But don't lose hope.
I made you most like gods except
for death, and eternity is not so far
from your reach as you think. If
instead of trashing your world, you
would set your mind to creating
heaven on earth, you too could achieve
that eternal boredom that you envy
the gods. So why don't you, instead
of giving me an eternal headache with
your eternal whining, become gods?
No plan is the best plan, I always say.
Except for family planning. We hate
overpopulation on Olympus. Think
what a trillion years of procreation
of eternal beings would do to this place.
That's why we neuter all male gods at
birth. I'm truly sorry, but I can't give you
another chance. I have written the perfect
program that only allows for
one chance to do things right and it
is my belief that you cannot do
better than perfect. You're on your
own folks. Trash yourselves or become gods. It's entirely up to you.

JASON
What proof of you can I give to man?
Men are such skeptics.

ZEUS
What need do you have of proofs? Do
I seem like a friendly chap who you
would go to tell about your car-
buncle? Do I whip down and save
people from sinking ships that've
stupidly run into icebergs? Do I
pluck idiots off the side of Mt
Everest when they get into trouble?

Whoops! Broke my own rule. That's
in the future. If you want proofs,
it's right in front of your nose.
Man has done everything he has set
out to do so far. Only a God could
do this. Man is a god, albeit a god
with a blessedly short life. What
proof of god does he need when he is
a god. Not wanting man to look like
something out of Star Trek, whoops,
there I went again, I made him in
my image, which is handsome, lacivious, drunken and infinitely devious.
Nof said? I'm out'a here. Next time
you pray, use a little imagination
and pray to a toad or a warthog.
You'll probably get just as good
results. I really hate all that
whining. (Exit deus ex machina)

JASON
I'm out'a here too. I wonder if I
am going to get a campaign ribbon
for this?

BARRY
(Hacking) You'll get the side of my
sword you swindler. A little more
trash can't hurt.

Lightening strikes his sword and he is hurled to his knees a supplicant to the Queen of Sparta.

BARRY
I meant no disrespect O Queen of
heaven.

QUEEN
O great boughs, oh straight and long
standing trunk, O manly countenance,
I come seeking the shelter of your

great strength. Yet the tyrant has
won the day. My husband to me, no
heed would pay. And now a terrible
deceit of peace has torn off his
branches and our brave Spartans lie
scattered limbs on this bloody monument to man's incarnation of hell.
Now our country dies, as our young
oaks crack and break and fall to
untimely deaths. The Athenians are
wolves in democracy's sheepskin.
Their greed incorporates the world.
My poor husband, a dull Spartan,
has paid the price of Athenian perfidy.
Why not listen, you men, when we women
speak. You only listen to your ideals,
who know you not half so well. How
should I feel? I hate all men of goodwill. The world vomits up their lives,
like a bitter pill. My daughter, a
practical man shall marry. One who
is glad to die in the arms of love.
Their families never want. Men of
ideals are like the strong oak. A
terrible wind does rip off their
branches and they do not budge.
KRUSHAMEMNON my dear. Where
are you my fine oak?

BARRY is still prostrate when his old adversary DIODOTUS
wanders by dressed in animal skins, having reverted to Stone Age life.
He chops on BARRY'S head with a stone ax thinking it an eatable
gourd.

>   BARRY
> What ho, I'm killed. Oh. It's only
> the shade of my old foe come to
> vex me. Where's my sword?

DIODOTUS

This is but a rotten gourd not worth
much. Sounds like empty words.
Wilderness wisdom, would you starve
me? My unnatural mother has deserted my plea. My civic love has
belched me from her breast, that
she may play frivolously. I her
conscience am now wild animal's
prey. Punish her I will, for now I
know that Sparta has the right and
Athens swine born tyranny. Still
I pray, and hope great ZEUS will
hear, that your hearts, your minds,
and your false policy will change,
that all good men, in good conscience may follow thee. Come down from
the high perch of your conceit and
see your folly, that all the world
is your enemy, or at best frightened
neutrality. Post a bail of ideas
that offer reality. I go with a
tear to participate in the death of
thee.

ARISTOPHENES

Human turds sit belching and farting
in the Athenian assembly. Virtue
gives her clean place to passion.
Industry has been replaced by repac-
ious greed. Flesh has replaced
leather as the chiefest raw material
of wealth. Where leather once was
sewn, flesh of man is hacked. Nothing
is more expendable than flesh except
to the loser of his skin. Yet our
democrats vote to skin our youth in
the interest of peace. It seems
better that we were cannibals, and
had some benefit of our youth, than

suffer such total waste. Yet these
men belch and fart their way through
their sessions devoid of a single
constructive thought. Man's suicidal
conspiracy with blind fools defies all
description. The words of the poet are
wasted on deaf ears. Great thoughts
have been replaced with great thoughts
of making money.

SOCRATES

Virtue is learned by a man in order
that he may pretend to be virtuous
and win the love of mankind. The
love of mankind is converted into
money and power and greatness. Soon
a son is born to the great man. It
is assumed that the son will not
only inherit great wealth, but will
also inherit the most priceless
treasure of all, virtue. Alas,
virtue, unlike wealth, cannot be in-
herited, and often the son born to
wealth and privilege becomes the
insolent hated greed of mankind.
The same fate befalls great nations,
for they too practiced virtue in
the beginning and became great.
But when this greatness turned into
tyranny, they earned the enmity of
all nations. The fate then of great
nations and great individuals is to
rise to power by virtue of hypocrisy,
since they cultivate virtue for
material gain, rather than for its
own sake. Thus Athens is going to
take a great fall, because she hasn't
learned virtue for its own sake.

DIANA

DIANA, THE HUNTRESS here again for
Eye of Zeus, your 24 hr. war channel.
300,000,000 people have died today
in various small wars throughout
the universe. Your great favorite
here in Greece has resumed after a
short truce. The cause of Athens
is safe for now. The island of
Sphagaie is reduced to rubble and
the entire population has been put
to the sword. There is mopping up
action taking place led by the great
hero BARRY who is personally giving
no quarter, as he dispatches women,
children and wounded. All is going
well for the forces of freedom and
democracy. The one mistake was that
catapult shot that hit the hospital.
Doctors there were studying the plague
which has now spread to the Athenian
army. (The messenger of the gods
MERCURY brings a news flash) Here's
some great breaking news. Sparta
and her allies have captured a large
island belonging to Athens. The
merciless rascals have put everyone
to death. First, they tormented
their captives by poring pepper in
the eyes. Oh well. What goes around
comes around. Humans will be humans.
I better hotfoot it out of here.
This war is getting down right dangerous.

BARRY

Another island gone! Are there no
end of islands? Is there no end of
islands? Which is correct is or are?
I must get back to my grammar. I

must resign this burgeoning generalship before I become as dumb as the
Spartans. I didn't ask for it. I
am a politician, a man of peace. It
was I who fought to the bitter end
for peace. Now another island falls.
This war will never end. I do not
care to fight these endless battles.
I am a simple orator. A counselor
to the people.

          HERCULES
Another island has been captured by
the Spartans. Let us triple our
arms production. Let us build a
thousand more ships. Bare the hills
of timber. There are plenty of cedars
in Lebanon. Scrape the bowels of
the earth clean of its metal. Arms,
arms, arms for the poor of the earth.
We shall be the richest nation in the
world.

KRUSH and JASON come together and fight. JASON is now wearing many campaign ribbons.
          KING
I see by your chest vile liar that
you participated in that vile mass-
acre at Sphagaie where you promised
peace.

          JASON
I am authorized to wear this ribbon,
but I didn't really participate.

          KING
Vile liar. If you were a man, you
would fall on your sword for being
a vile fraud.

JASON
May the gods be my witness, I am
fully justified in killing you.
Sparta has spurned Athens generous
peace offer and renewed her ungen-
erous aggressions. It is you who
are the vile liar and your calumny
about my ribbons is the last straw.

KING
You Athenians, by your actions which
don't fit your words, have cursed
yourselves to eternal war.

JASON
In what truce have you ever kept
your word? Die king of liars.

They stab each other simultaneously and both die.

JASON & KRUSH
(Together) I die! Long live Hellas.

The wives both arrive at the scene to find their dying husbands in their
death agony. They stare at each other in disbelief and
fall on each other weeping.

BARRY
It is too late to turn back now.
We must fight on to the death. There
is no other option. One would have
to be a fool to trust the Spartans.
I have set in motion the invisible
hand of ZEUS. Let each man cheat
and steal from his fellow man equally. Survival of the most ruthless
and rotten is the way of nature. An
intelligent animal like man must
destroy his enemies with high ideals.
I have done very well by co-opting

the myth of democracy. The mob should
be grateful to have an opportunity
to do as well. A caution to the wise.
Do not be fooled by effete words like
love. Only a fool would love his
neighbor and give him a chance to rob
him blind. Democracy can be destroyed
by such subversive ideas. The Spartans
must be destroyed to the last man.
Everything must be turned into armament.
We should even re-open the quarries.
Stone weapons were once used quite
effectively. That will make a great
campaign slogan. Back to the stone
age with BARRY. But I forgot, I am
dictator for life.

Tumultuous roar of the mob.

MOB
BARRY! BARRY! BARRY! DICTATOR!

CURTAIN

MARSHALL'S AGENCY

A one-act comedy

Written by

Ed Wode

Copyright © 1999
By Ed Wode
edwode@gmail.com

MARSHALL'S AGENCY

MAIN CHARACTERS

MARSHALL MACPHERSON - A roly-poly devil may care, somewhat irresponsible, child-like individual who in his own eyes is the opposite of all these shortcomings. His "agency" is not only supposed to obtain jobs for actors, but to save them from the evils of the world. It specializes in handicapped and quirky individuals.

JANE - The long suffering erratically paid secretary of the agency. She is cute, terse, hard, efficient and all business. Don't expect any favoritism here. She rides herd on Marshall who kids her about being under worked and overpaid.

LARRY - A tall, thin, blond black man, very trendy in every way like the well known black basketball star who is always in trouble. He is Marshall's agent stooge who never gets a proper update from Marshall and is therefore misinformed about many "Agency" matters.

DR. GOLDEN - He is a ninety-year-old health fanatic who owns a juice bar-restaurant in addition to being a medical doctor. He's comically cagey, playing senile when it suits him to get what he wants. He has become a backer of the "Agency" to help pretty starving actresses stay healthy.

ED RIZZOLI - Ed is a reformed TAGGER who, after Hollywood bought his life story, has become a screenwriter. He is the "Agency's" most successful writer.

SUSIE DEWSIE - She is a terminally pretty actress who has become an actress to help overcome her stuttering.

GEORGETTE - She is an overweight, flashy "fire head" who is willing to do anything it takes to become a star, especially sleep with PRODUCERS or DIRECTORS.

KEN KLIPER - He is a killer-handsome actor who is totally irresponsibly addicted to seducing every female actress he can.

CRISSY WELLS - A teen-age look-alike actress who falls for Ken until she finds out how shallow and insincere he is.

MARSHALL'S AGENCY

A Comedy

CAST OF CHARACTERS

MARSHALL MACPHERSON - Agency head.

JANE - Agency secretary.

LARRY LONGHEART - Agent assistant to Marshall.

DR. GOLDEN - Agency backer

KEN KLIPPER - Agency rep'd actor.

GEORGETTE - Agency rep'd actor.

SUSIE - Agency rep'd actor

ED RIZZOLI - Agency rep'd writer.

CRISSY WELLS - Agency rep'd actor.

MARSHALL'S AGENCY

A Comedy

Scene 1.

The office of MacPherson Actor's and Writer's Agency about 9:30AM. There are three desks in the office, which is shared by MARSHALL MacPHERSON head of the agency, his secretary JANE and LARRY LONGHART his trusted assistant. LARRY and JANE are hard at work fielding phone calls that are mostly for the two hour late as usual, MARSHALL.

       JANE
   (Answers phone) "Marshall's Agency."
   (Beat) No, we do not do evictions.
   We are an actors and writers agency.

JANE hangs up just as MARSHALL enters.

       JANE
   Where in the world have you been?
   20th Century Fox has been calling
   all morning about that script of ED'S
   they can't find.

       LARRY
   Yes, I took five calls. They want you
   to rush another right away. That
   happy hit man aids script is a hot
   topic right now.

       JANE
   Yes, the only thing hotter than gang-
   ster germ scripts are dumb scripts
   and they think Ed has both bases
   covered.

       MARSHALL
   ED'S a dumb genius, Jane. Who else

would have thought of a vampire hit
man in this age of aids?

                    LARRY
          But who's gonna play that part boss?

                    MARSHALL
          Go buy some teeth LARRY. This may be
          your big break.

LARRY, who is black, turns ashen as a ghost at the thought.

                    LARRY
          I'll stick to being an agent boss.

                    JANE
          ED'S script MARSHALL. Where is it?

                    MARSHALL
          Oh God JANE. ED is going to kill me.
          He went on vacation and I told him I
          have plenty of scripts.

                    JANE
          Well, don't you.

MARSHALL opens a closet filled with scripts and they fall into room.

                    MARSHALL
          There's over ten thousand scripts
          there, but none of ED'S I can find.
           (Opens a small fridge) And I keep
          his in a special place - next to the
          herring in the refrigerator.

                    JANE
          Have you looked on your desk?

MARSHALL
There you go you slave driver. You
expect me to find anything there?

The desk is knee deep in paper. JANE and MARSHALL begin to sort
frantically through the mess heaving paper in all directions.

JANE
It's got to be here somewhere.

LARRY
(Helping) This is why normal agencies
have mailrooms.

MARSHALL
Yes, but they have normal employees.

JANE
Here's one.

MARSHALL
Oh, thank God JANE. You may have
saved my life. You know how ED got
his big break?

JANE
By battering his pet mongoose and

getting you to sell the story?

MARSHALL
Close. He used to be a top tagger
until they shot him in the knee with
a BB gun for not paying his dues to the
Tagger's Benevolent Assoc.

JANE
So what?

MARSHALL
He got the Union officers addresses
and tagged their houses.

JANE
So that's how he became a national
hero and sold his first script.

LARRY
Your house might be an improvement
boss with some of ED'S artwork.

MARSHALL
(Sitting at LARRY'S neat clean desk)
Now that I can breathe easier, I think I like
this desk better. You can have mine
Gumby.

JANE
(Leafing through script) Well don't
breathe easy too soon. Half the pages
are ruined. Coffee stains, ketchup
and the rest I think somebody ate a
hot fudge Sunday off of.

LARRY
I saw you eating one yesterday boss.

MARSHALL
You snitch LARRY. O.K., O.K. I know
it's my fault. Send it to the laundry
with the money.

JANE
We don't have those backers anymore.

MARSHALL
See, I knew it was a mistake when you
made me get an honest backer.

JANE
They picked the perfect way to make money disappear. Are you aware you owe me two months salary and three months overtime?

MARSHALL
As long as I owe you, you're never going to be broke.

Enter SUSIE DEWSIE

SUSIE
(Stuttering badly) MR. Mc, Mc, Mc. PHERSON! What a surprise ca, ca, ca, catching you in.

MARSHALL
I'm a little surprised to be here so early myself, SUSIE. Are you still starring in, "As the World Stutters?"

SUSIE
Yes, but the show is being canceled next week. Can you get me another show?

MARSHALL
Sure. LARRY, see that you find SUSIE another show. There's a lot of new lesbian shows. See if stuttering is acceptable behavior.

SUSIE
But MR. Mc, Mc, Mc, Mc, Mc. (Can't stop)

MARSHALL
I knew you'd be excited SUSIE. Call us next week. And wear a bib to the interviews.

SUSIE
But, but, but, but, but, but...

LARRY has to help her to the door and she exits almost in tears.

JANE
There goes another valuable client.

MARSHALL
Don't worry. She's got about as much chance of getting another gig as I have of getting cast as Rhett Butler in a re-make of Gone With the Wind.

JANE
It depends on which wind the movie is about.

MARSHALL
(Mock anger) I can't wait until our new backer DR. GOLDEN gets here with my check. I'm going to have lunch for the rest of the day.

JANE
Like you need it with that waist.

MARSHALL
I can't wait to escape this haven for twenty-first century penis envy.

JANE
You try to sneak off and leave me with all the casting for this agency and you won't have to worry about penis envy when I get through.

She picks up the scissors threateningly

MARSHALL
(Stutters) Ca, ca, ca, calm down JANE.
Ya, ya, ya know I care about SUSIE,
LARRY. I stutter myself sometimes.
Let me see those casting sheets.
Here's one that's perfect for you
JANE. They're doing a commercial for
safe sex starring Tarzan and Jane sky
diving with the same chute. He wears a red
white and blue condom ripcord and you
give the ripcord a pull until the chute opens.
And Larry can be the parachute packer-diving
instructor. As in deep sea that is.

LARRY and JANE blow up.

JANE & LARRY
I quit.

MARSHALL
Now wait a minute. You can't quit.
I owe you both three months salary.
LARRY you take all the calls while
JANE and I do the casting sheets.

LARRY
But all the calls are for you.

MARSHALL
Well there you are. You help JANE.
I'm glad you understand me LARRY.

LARRY
I understand you perfectly. That's
why I have the paramedics standing by
with a straightjacket.

MARSHALL
You know you are my favorite agent

LARRY even if you are my only agent. And I love you too JANE. The three of us are the perfect business menage-a-trois.

JANE
This is too much. Maybe we better call 911 LARRY and report him for sexual harassment before this gets any thicker.

The phone rings and LARRY answers.

LARRY
It's for you boss. It's PHIL at 20th Century Fox.

MARSHALL
(Answers) PHIL ole buddy. How are you. We don't have a copy of that script PHIL. Somebody used ED'S script as a foot mat. We have two, but they both look the same.

JANE
Is he out of his mind talking to 20th like that?

MARSHALL
You'll double the offer PHIL? (Marshall covers phone speaker) What a negotiator I am.

JANE has her head in hands.

LARRY
The lord works in mysterious ways JANE.

JANE
I think the word is absurd LARRY.

LARRY
That's what I meant.

JANE
He could at least get to work on time
when we are auditioning animals. I
had to baby sit an orangutan so
long before MARSHALL got here yesterday,
he began to sexually harass me. And
I want to tell you, the way he was hung,
I hesitated a good 30 seconds before
I called my lawyer.

LARRY
You have all the luck JANE.

JANE
Why doesn't he become a preacher with
all that hot air about love?

LARRY
Religion has enough contradictions
already.

MARSHALL
Larry, where's ED?

LARRY
South America.

MARSHALL
(To LARRY & JANE) Why doesn't somebody tell me what's going on here?

To PHIL on phone.

ED is on vacation for a month in
South America... in the jungle where
there aren't any phones.

JANE
(To LARRY) We have his itinerary and
a satellite phone number right here.
Somebody wake him up.

LARRY
It's called negotiating JANE. Calm
down.

MARSHALL
I'm not playing hard to get PHIL.
Make a big enough offer and I'll get
ED back to town even if I have to
lead a safari to do it. And I hate
snakes even worse than starving actors.

JANE
Did you read the contract he signed
with DR. GOLDEN?

LARRY
No, but MARSHAL assured me that he
took that ninety-nine year old health
nut to the cleaners... (Beat) spiri-
tually speaking of course. This is
a noble cause for DR. GOLDEN, no
matter what the sacrifice.

JANE
Maybe we should order him a coffin.

MARSHALL
I do not put tracking devices on my
artists PHIL. They are not criminals.
Maybe a few are like ED. (Beat) Phil,
if you want ED to paint graffiti on
the statue of liberty to promote this
project, I wash my hands of it... (Beat)
An extra mil... Maybe we can talk about
it over a power lunch sometime.

JANE
(Reading contract) You know what that dirty old health nut is up to? He's going to have all the casting couches in the offices monitored by close circuit T.V. supervised by himself. I may never be able to flirt again.

LARRY
This is just unsophisticated contract language Jane.

JANE
(Beginning to cry) And some of those actors are cute.

LARRY
Don't worry JANE. Between our interest and MARSHALL'S interest we own a majority of the stock. You have my permission to flirt. Let him play with himself all day long if he pays our salaries.

JANE
(Drying eyes) It says here that DR. GOLDEN owns 51 percent and MARSHALL owns 49 percent. Nothing about us owning anything. GOLDEN'S the real boss now. Do you realize that?

LARRY
I always knew MARSHALL couldn't add two and two and have it come out to four. But this is at my expense. I won't stand for it.

JANE
Looks like our chickens already been plucked LARRY.

LARRY
That dirty old con artist has taken
MARSHALL to the cleaners.

JANE
And we just got rid of the Laundromat!

LARRY
If he puts a camera on me, he'll be
looking at the moon.

MARSHALL still talking to PHIL at the desk across the room.

MARSHALL
What's the bottom line PHIL? 1 mil?

Covers the phone with hand and yells.

$1,000,000.

Repeats loudly over phone.

$1,000,000! You bet we'll take it.
(Beat) As soon as I check with my
client. Thank you PHIL. I'm off
to the tropics on the first flight.

MARSHALL starts to sing.

We're in the money, we're in the
money.

To JANE and LARRY.

ED'S script is sold for $1,000,000
American money as soon as we have
his approval. Get ED on the phone.
Get ED on the phone. I got 'a tell
him the good news.

JANE
(Looking at itinerary) He's in the
Galapagos Islands betting on the
turtle races.

MARSHALL
Turtle races? I don't care if it's
snail races. Get him on the phone.
Find him now.

JANE
Right away. By the way. Here's
your copy of the contract you signed
with GOLDEN. Should I file it?

MARSHALL
No. I haven't had time to look at
it yet.

JANE and LARRY look at each other in shocked surprise.

JANE & LARRY
You mean you haven't read it?

MARSHALL
No. We discussed all the details.
Signing was just a formality.

JANE & LARRY
Read it!

JANE hands the contract to Marshall just as DR. GOLDEN enters all smiles. Marshall sits there with contract in hand reading.

DR. GOLDEN
Hello everybody. Hard at work I see.
Have we any problems today?

A moving company is following DOCTOR GOLDEN with furnishings.

Come right this way gentlemen.

              MARSHALL

What's going on Doc? We didn't discuss anything about decorating. And what are the T.V. cameras for? Are we setting up a studio?

              DR. GOLDEN

MARSHALL, don't you read your contracts? We are going to completely redecorate these offices.

              MARSHALL

Wait, stop now. Contract or no contract, I choose the furniture in my offices.

              LARRY

Not anymore. (Looking at contract) It says here, no more bar, no more frig and you will be here at your new pink desk at 8 A.M. sharp after eating your oat bran and running five miles.

              MARSHALL

I thought communism was dead.

              JANE

It is, but it's been replaced with Fascism.

              DR. GOLDEN

(Gives movers directions) Move all that stuff into the back office. Set up the wheat grass machine, the water ionizer, the juice extracter, my examining table and find a good place for the wheatgrass. We are going to have the healthiest actors in America. Get rid of the booze.

When the movers hear this they wink at each other and quickly move toward the other room. MARSHALL, who has now read most of the contract, goes ballistic.

> MARSHALL
> You raped me without ever kissing me DR. GOLDEN. Come here and let's make love and get this straightened out right now. This is not how we discussed things.

> DR. GOLDEN
> I'm sorry MARSHALL, but this is what the lawyer drew up to protect my investment. If you don't like it, I will be a gentleman and withdraw my backing. I could never want to force anyone into a deal they couldn't live with. I think you tried to take a little advantage of me, so I turned the tables on you.

DR. GOLDEN sticks his tongue out at MARSHALL.

> MARSHALL
> I'm a man of my word DR. GOLDEN. But it should be a fifty-fifty deal. I don't mind having you as a full partner, but I don't think you know enough about this business to call it your cup of prune juice yet. That's the best I can live with. Half a cup of prune juice is better than a full cup unless you're sitting on the toilet. We'll use the CAMERAS for actors demo tapes. No big brother here.

> DR. GOLDEN
> That's the deal I had in mind. I don't know what the lawyer drew up. I don't

read contracts either.

LARRY and JANE give knowing looks to each other.

>   MARSHALL
> Good. And you can have the back office
> for your hi-colonic juice bar.

>   DR. GOLDEN
> And you get the first colonic free MARSHALL.
> And all the wheat grass you can drink.

MARSHALL starts to barf.

>   MARSHALL
> As long as I am boss.

>   LARRY
> That's fine for you two, but what
> about honoring my 10% stock option?

>   DR. GOLDEN
> Stock options? I like that idea.

>   MARSHALL
> Honor what?

>   LARRY
> You promised me 10% for not telling
> your wife about that actress you
> gave mouth to mouth resuscitation too
> when she almost drowned doing that
> bubble bath commercial we were
> monitoring to protect her from peeping
> producers.

>   MARSHALL
> If the old dreadnought would have
> found out I'd be dead. But that was
> the old company. You can have the

whole thing.

            LARRY
I guess you give me no other choice...

            DR. GOLDEN
I'll honor your stock options if
MARSHALL will. I know he overlooked
it by mistake. And what about JANEY?
Shouldn't she have 10% too?

            MARSHALL
(With mock anger) Now just a minute.
If you want to give LARRY 10%, JANE
10% and maybe the janitor a percent,
you can give it out of your 50%. And
besides, females are suppose to work
and not be heard from.

JANE lets out a karate yell and is about to give MARSHALL a kick from hell.

            MARSHALL
(Stutters) O. K, K, K, K... DR. GOLDEN.
I was just kidding. LARRY should have
10% and JANE too. They do all the
work around here anyway.

The phone rings and JANE answers it. She is sweet now.

            JANE
MARSHALL, I've got ED on the phone
from the Galapagos Islands.

            MARSHALL
(Nice & smooth) How's the vacation
chief. We've missed our resident
killer of a tagger. (Beat) Writer
I meant.

Lights up on another area of the stage where ED is on other end of telephone line in a hospital bed. His head is in bandages and the bandages muffle his voice. This is a 3-way conference call with Ed's doctor also on line. The doctor is not seen.

       ED
(Muffled) What do you want?

      MARSHALL
Is somebody sitting on your face? I can't seem to make out a word you're saying.

       ED
I'm in a jungle hospital.

      MARSHALL
(Alarmed) What! In a jungle hospital? (Beat) Got bit by a giant turtle? (Beat) At least, did you win the race? (Beat) You did. In the turtle's mouth! (Beat) You got to get out of the hospital and get back here right away. Fox is offering 1 mil. for your happy hit man script as soon as we deliver a script. (Beat) We don't have one. (Beat) There was an earthquake and the herring fell on it. (Beat) My house is fine. Why? (Beat) I like it the way it is. (Beat) You got to get back here even on a stretcher. (Beat) Do you understand $1,000,000, not pesos, American money? (Beat) You don't have to tag anybody... although we might be able to make a deal... (Beat) You want me to give the turtle a contract? Oh, put a contract on the turtle? Forget that turtle. It's probably dead from food poisoning by now. (beat) There's no honor in whacking a turtle. Let me talk to your doctor.

                        Ed
It's a conference call Marshall. Tell him Doc.

                    MARSHALL
What! You're going to keep him under
observation for another week? I don't
care if he has rabies, I want him
back in L.A. tomorrow. (Beat) He does?
Put a muzzle on him and send him anyway. (Beat) If you do me this favor, I'll
hire you as my gardener. In L.A. you'll
make more money in an hour as a gardener
than you do in that jungle in a year as a
doctor. Deal? Put ED back on. (Beat)
ED, it worked. I'll see you in 24 hrs
And if you got rabies, try not to foam
at the mouth when we pick up the
check. (Beat) They'll think we are
hungry and offer us less the next
time. Good-bye chief. (beat) JANE, I'm
going back and see if the good DR. has
anything stronger to drink than carrot juice.
ED is threatening to blow up my house
if this deal falls through. Come on
LARRY. You're buying.

Exit MARSHALL and LARRY. Enter GEORGETTE, an actress represented by the agency. She has bright red hair and is voluptuously built. She has her nose stuck in the air and her butt stuck out. She wears very revealing micro-minis. She is here ostensibly to see MARSHALL, but her real intention is to sneak a look at the casting notices and make her own appointments.

                    GEORGETTE
Hi, JANE. Why so glum? Is MARSHALL
being a bad boy again?

JANE gives GEORGETTE an icy stare and answers the phone.

JANE
(On phone) We are looking for an
actress 18 or older that can pass
for a pregnant teenager. (Beat) No,
you don't have to get pregnant, but
it wouldn't hurt if you were. Knowing this director you might end
up that way. (Beat) You're 18, going on 15.
Perfect. Come in tomorrow at 10 A.M.
And look innocently trashy.

Hangs up and confronts GEORGETTE.

Speaking of 25 and going on 8, how
are you GEORGETTE?

GEORGETTE
I'd be perfect for that part.

JANE
Mentally you're a little too young
and physically you look like the
typical worn out 25-year-old Hollywood nymphomaniac.

GEORGETTE
I want to see MARSHALL. He promised me three interviews this week
and I haven't heard a word from him.
He only sees me when I am doing
underwear commercials.

JANE
He's in an important meeting. (A
scream) Did you have an appointment
or did you just come over to give away
VICTORIA'S secrets?

GEORGETTE
You know it's a waste of time making
an appointment with MARSHALL, because he never keeps them.

JANE
That's rotten, but the truth. Wait
here.

Blackout on this area, lights up on area of Dr. Golden's office.

JANE exits and GEORGETTE goes and looks at the breakdowns and takes notes. DR. GOLDEN enters, doing a double take when he sees GEORGETTE bending over the casting notices. He continues into his office where JANE is complaining to MARSHALL about GEORGETTE. MARSHALL is lying on the examining table with LARRY fanning him. He drank something labeled rye whisky that DR. GOLDEN used for one of his health juice cocktails and has become ill as a result.

JANE
Marshall, sometimes I wonder whether
you are an agent or a pimp. GEORGETTE
is here to see you.

MARSHALL
My head, my stomach, my feet, I drank
something labeled rye whisky and it was
poison. I'm going to die.

JANE
What are you going to do about that
low rider bate?

MARSHALL
Is this Tuesday? I always give her
new underwear approval on Tuesdays.
Why don't you melt down and get some
VICTORIA'S SECRET stuff yourself?
You might turn out to be human.

JANE
You think it might help me land one
of our cute actors?

MARSHALL
(Holding head) I doubt it, but DR.
GOLDEN would probably perk up.

JANE furious, storms out of the office, as DR. GOLDEN is entering, almost knocking him over.

DR. GOLDEN
Did I hear somebody mention my name?

MARSHALL
Yes, I was just saying how good it is
to have someone around the office who
JANE can relate to.

DR. GOLDEN
That ice cube? I prefer that fire-
head I saw when I came in.

MARSHALL
Oh, you mean GEORGETTE the red menace?

DR. GOLDEN
I thought it was QUEEN VICTORIA re-

vealing her secrets.

MARSHALL
I can see you stay on top of things
DR. GOLDEN.

DR. GOLDEN
I like the bottom just as well.

MARSHALL
What kind of rye whisky was this stuff?

I'm not feeling too great.

>   DR. GOLDEN
> That wasn't whisky, it was hemlock,
> a deadly poison. (MARSHALL screams)
> Don't worry Marshall, I have the perfect
> anecdote.

Blackout on this area, lights up on main office area.

JANE enters the main office and sees GEORGETTE looking at the casting notices and goes totally ballistic.

>   JANE
> GEORGETTE you sneak! You have no
> right to look at those casting not-
> ices. This agency could lose its
> license. Give me those notes you
> made.

>   GEORGETTE
> How else do you expect me to get work?
> I haven't been sent on an interview
> since "Nympho Behind Bars". And the
> director was behind bars or I would
> have stood on my head to get that part.

>   JANE
> The way you wear your dresses you
> don't have to. (There is a blood
> curdling scream and MARSHALL rushes
> in.) My, God! What's wrong boss?

>   MARSHALL
> I drank hemlock whisky and the doctor
> wants to amputate my feet.

>   JANE
> But why?

MARSHALL
Hemlock poisons the feet first.

JANE
You know, this might be a big improvement. When you take your shoes off, even the rattlesnakes run for cover.

MARSHALL
I'm dying. Call the paramedics.

DR. GOLDEN enters with a chain saw and MARSHALL screams.

MARSHALL
Get that B movie maniac away from me.

DR. GOLDEN
I was just playing a joke on you MARSHALL, because you drank my favorite Brussels Sprout juice. And this chain saw is only to cut up your old desk.

MARSHALL
Let me check that gizmo out DOC.

MARSHALL takes it from the doctor and turns it on. He slices a fresh pineapple plant the Doctor has given Jane. DR. GOLDEN pleads with him to stop.

MARSHALL
DOC, if you touch my desk, your head is going to look like this pineapple.

JANE
A slice of pineapple anyone except Georgette. Boss, Georgette was sneaking again...

DR. GOLDEN
Come on Marshall. Let's go drink a toast to

live and let live. I have a bottle of natural
Champaign in my office.

MARSHALL
Now you're cooking partner. Why don't you
two try to be more supportive of each other
while I take care of partner bonding duties?

Blackout this area and up on back office. Marshall and the Doctor have just toasted.

MARSHALL
Wow! That was natural? Natural isn't as bad
as I thought it was.

DR. GOLDEN
You're an instant convert eh Marshall? I have
some fermented potato juice too Marshall.

MARSHALL
Conversion to one religion at a time is
my motto Doc. I can handle an encore
glass of holy bubble water if you're not saving it
for New Years Eve. (Doc fills his glass and
as he starts to drink there is a loud commotion
from the main office.) What's all that commotion?

There are screams from the other office that cause MARSHALL to spill his drink as he rushes to find out what is going on. JANE is sitting on GEORGETTE pulling her hair. When MARSHALL sees this, he thinks he has a lesbian office affair on his hands and assumes calm authority.

MARSHALL
What's going on ladies? I know I said to
be more supportive, but I didn't say to
start rehearsing for one of those new gay
TV series?

JANE
GEORGETTE helped herself to the cast-
in breakdowns again.

MARSHALL
GEORGETTE, you should know by now
that fire heads always get caught.

GEORGETTE
You promised me if I went on three
calls a week, I'd be a star, but this
geek never sends me out.

MARSHALL
You are an underwear star.

JANE
On the casting director's couch.

GEORGETTE grabs JANE'S hair and begins to pull. MARSHALL tries to intervene but gets the worst of it as he is kicked, scratched and bit. When he gets them apart he pleads on bended knee.

MARSHALL
Ladies, ladies, we are supposed to
be loving of one another in this
agency. Ouch! You bit me GEORGETTE.
Ouch! You kicked me JANE. Stop,
stop. GEORGETTE!

GEORGETTE
You are banned from my underwear
commercials from now on MARSHALL

MARSHALL
(On bended knee) JANE, please see
that GEORGETTE goes on three calls
every week.

JANE

There aren't that many parts for sluts.

              MARSHALL
I admit it's my fault. I'll work
smarter from now on.

DR. GOLDEN enters.

              DR. GOLDEN
What's all the commotion now? Every
five minutes I have to turn down my
remote hearing aid.

              MARSHALL
This is our new backer DR. GOLDEN, Georgette. DR. GOLDEN, I want you to meet one of our prettiest actresses, GEORGETTE.

              GEORGETTE
You cute little old man. Why don't
you take me away from this horrible
place and buy me a drink?

DR. GOLDEN'S eyes are bugging out of his head. He tidies his hair, licks his lips and with lust in his heart:

              DR. GOLDEN
I'd be glad to, as long as it's carrot
juice for me.

GEORGETTE takes his arm and they exit.

              MARSHALL
Saved by young love.

SUSIE DEWSIE enters.

              MARSHALL
Here's more trouble. How was

that beer commercial SUSIE? I
hear they gave you enough Spudweiser
to make you pee for a year.

                    SUSIE
          Here's your 10% commission Marshall.

SUSIE gives him a roll of toilet paper.

                    MARSHALL
          LARRY, see if you can get her an
          ex-lax commercial. I'll supply them
          with toilet paper and make a fortune.

SUSIE flounces out in a huff.

                    JANE
          Can we get back to the breakdowns?
          Here's a part that's perfect for
          GEORGETTE. "69 Minutes Over Mancho
          Pincho", co-starring somebody named BUNDY.

                    MARSHALL
          AL BUNDY?

                    JANE
          No, his cannibal mentor TED BUNDY.
          And here's one called "Jaws at Camelot".
          They want an actor who will joust with
          a great white shark wearing a suit of armor.
          Ken would be perfect.

                    MARSHALL
          Can he swim? Yes, send Ken Klipper; we
          have him insured for a million or will if he
          gets the part.

                    JANE
          And here's a commercial for subliminal

political advertising on toilet tissue.
Perfect for SUSIE.

              MARSHALL
What's the subliminal message on the
toilet paper?

              JANE
Get off your ass and vote.

              MARSHALL
It ought to be wipe your ass with the nearest
politician.

Dr. Golden enters carrying a large picture of a nude woman.

              MARSHALL
That was a fast drink Dr. Golden.

              DR. GOLDEN
Georgette became ill when she tasted
the carrot juice martini. I offered to
exam her, but she said she was going to
the ER and try out for a part with a
cute intern.

              MARSHALL
Where'd you get that picture DR.
GOLDEN? This is an actor's agency,
not a nudie bar.

              DR. GOLDEN
This is paint by numbers fine art. When you're
bored, you can paint her underwear on and I'll
go monitor Georgette's commercials for you. This
goes right over your desk.

              MARSHALL
You fix up my office anyway you want

> DR. GOLDEN. No beds allowed by SAG rules, but collapsible wheelchairs are.

> DR. GOLDEN
> How about two-inch thick shag carpets and big stuffy pillows?

> MARSHALL
> For a ninety-year old holistic health doctor, you sure got a strong yen, DR. GOLDEN. Maybe I should try some of that rabbit food you eat.

> DR. GOLDEN
> I'd be more than happy to share my Brussels Sprouts MARSHALL

> MARSHALL
> I'm not feeling too well Jane. I'm going to the bank to deposit DR. GOLDEN'S check and have a light lunch. I'll see you in the morning. Hold ED'S hand for me if he gets here before I do. Red meat here I come.

DR. GOLDEN shakes his head sadly and JANE disgustedly looks at her hand.

> JANE
> (Looking at hand) Yuck.

> DR. GOLDEN
> Red meat! I must save MARSHALL

DR. GOLDEN calls his bank and puts a hold on his check.

> DR. GOLDEN
> Hello, I want to stop a check. Reason? To save the rain forest.

Blackout, end of scene one.

Scene 2
Agency office next morning.

JANE and LARRY are at their desks fielding calls as usual. KEN KLIPER, one of the agencies young actors enters. Ken is a ruthless womanizer.

> KEN
> Hello everybody, I'm here for the
> weekly sermon on the mount. Where's
> all the new talent?

> LARRY
> Hello KEN. Nobody's here yet, but the
> boss wants to see you.

> KEN
> If he ever gets here. Right?

CRISSY WELLS the teenage look-alike enters.

> CRISSY
> Hello. I'm CRISSY WELLS. I'm here
> to try out for the part of a pregnant
> teenager.

> JANE
> Mr. MacPHERSON isn't in yet. Take
> these sides and look them over in
> the conference room. Mr. MacPHERSON
> should be here any minute.

> KEN
> Yeah, right. I'll help you learn the
> part CRISSY. I'm KEN KLIPER one of
> this agencies best actors. I've got
> to wait for MARSHALL anyway.

JANE
MR. KLIPER. You presume too much.

KEN
You're friendly today. What'sa matter?
Somebody pull your hair?

JANE
(Takes out mirror and looks) No.

LARRY
Run lines with CRISSY, KEN, but don't
mess up that conference room. Got it?

JANE
Be sure to wait KEN. The boss has
a part made in heaven for you.

LARRY
You're a natural for this one KEN.

KEN
Come on CRISSY. I know where the conference room is. I'll have you in
shape by the time MARSHALL arrives,
believe me.

Exit KEN and CRISSY.

JANE
I don't know whether that was a good
idea LARRY.

LARRY
There's no casting couch.

JANE
Just a big conference table.

LARRY
Covered with DR. GOLDEN'S wheat grass plantation.

JANE
Haven't you heard of the movie, "Splendor in the Grass"?

LARRY
Did you say grass? I better go...

They are distracted from this reality by the noise of a wheelchair containing ED RIZZOLI. ED enters with a cast on his foot and a bandage on his head. Maybe a muzzle on his mouth.

ED
Hi JANE. I'm back.

JANE
MR. RIZZOLI! ED! You poor man. Did one turtle do all that?

ED
Those turtles are as big as tanks.

MARSHALL enters.

MARSHALL
Chief, you're back. How'd you get back so fast looking like a mummy dog?

ED
Jets go fast MARSHALL.

MARSHALL
I wouldn't know. I'm afraid of heights. JANE, get me PHIL SPECTOR on the phone right away.

                    ED
        Can't wait to get your hands on my
        money can you MARSHALL?

MARSHALL grabs ED out of the wheelchair and dances him around
the room singing.

                    MARSHALL
        (Singing) We're in the money, we're
        in the money...

                    JANE
        PHIL SPECTOR'S office on the phone.

                    MARSHALL
        (On phone) This is MARSHALL MacPHER-
        SON. May I speak to PHIL? He's
        expecting my call. (Beat) What! Are
        you kidding?

ED starts to get fidgety.

        Aright, have him call me if you
        hear from him. (Hangs up)

                    ED
        What do you mean if they hear from him?
        He works there doesn't he?

                    MARSHALL
        ED, there's going to be a slight delay.
        PHIL has been fired and will be
        out of touch for a while. He'll call
        us soon as he gets back from the Amazon.

ED who has been pouting, turns red with anger and throws a fit.

                    ED
        I knew it. First vacation in five
        years and you ruin it.

MARSHALL is almost in tears. Ed continues.

>You told me it was sold yesterday.
>What is this, some joke? (Beat)
>I could be back there turtle watching
>in paradise while I'm recovering
>from my wounds. I could be hugging all
>the green party females hugging
>trees. No pollution, no noise, no headaches,
>and now no peace of mind. I might as well
>have gone to see my UNCLE RIZZOLI in
>Sing Sing where he is directing a play I wrote,
>called "Nympho Behind Bars."

>MARSHALL

ED please chief, please calm down.
Listen, I'll, I'll send you back to
the Galapagos. JANE can go with you,
if you like ice cubes.

>JANE

Ice cubes. Are you hot ED? You poor
man. I'll get you some ice.

>ED

You bet I'm hot, but I'll settle for
a bowl of turtle soup for lunch. No
ice cubes like JANE.

>JANE

I wouldn't go anyway.

>MARSHALL

Lunch is on me. Let's go everybody.

>JANE

Me too?

>MARSHALL

Yeah, we three.

LARRY
Me four?

MARSHALL
You guard the wealth Gumby. I'll
give you a raise instead.

LARRY
I'll settle for getting paid.

MARSHALL
That's what I meant.

Enter the Doctor.

DR. GOLDEN
Are we rehearsing a porno movie in
the conference room?

JANE & LARRY simultaneously.

JANE & LARRY
KEN and CRISSY!

MARSHALL
We don't do porno movies DOC. Maybe
you ate the wrong kind of mushrooms.

JANE
They're waiting for you in the conference room MARSHALL.

MARSHALL
I'd rather have a steak. Let's go Ed.

JANE
KEN KLIPER & CRISSY WELLS are
waiting.

MARSHALL
Why didn't you say so? Yes I want

to say good-bye to KEN. But who is
CRISSY WELLS?

     JANE
The newly pregnant teenager. I mean...

    MARSHALL
I think I know what you mean. I don't
mind my actors being martyrs, but
sex in this office will get them the
death penalty.

He rushes down the hall. VO offstage.

    MARSHALL (VO)
KEN and CRISSY stop that. Some
people drink that grass.

     DR. GOLDEN
You're all invited to lunch. There's
plenty of brussels sprouts for
everyone.

MARSHALL comes rushing back.

     JANE
I told you it would be "Bordello
In the Grass", LARRY.

     LARRY
"Bordello in the Grass". Great name
idea boss.

    MARSHALL
And you can be the Madame Larry

CRISSY and KEN come in straightening their clothes.

MARSHALL
Well what do you have to say for
yourselves?

KEN
I was teaching CRISSY Papal
method acting.

MARSHALL
It looked more like Papal roulette
to me.

CRISSY
He tricked me. I wish you were dead
KEN KLIPER.

MARSHALL
Good thinking CRISSY. KEN, all will be
forgiven if you get the part in "Jaws
at Camelot" I am sending you on. And
CRISSY, I can see you're a natural
for a pregnant teenager. LARRY, the
three of us are going to lunch. See
if you can part these two long enough
to get them a part in a movie. This
agency can't make money unless it's
actors are working. Come on ED. Come
on JANE.

All three exit the office helping Ed hobble along arm in arm having a little trouble getting out the door.

LARRY
O.K. you two. Here's your calls. Now,
 get out of my sight. (They exit hand
in hand as LARRY answers phone)
"MARSHALL'S AGENCY" (Angry) No,
no, no, we don't do evictions. (Slams down
the phone and assumes a crestfallen
look.) But maybe we should.

Blackout on office area, lights up on restaurant area. Just a couple of chairs and a table with a checkered cloth will do.

MARSHALL, JANE and ED are sitting at the table having just finished lunch. MARSHALL starts fumbling in his wallet for his credit card

                MARSHALL
(Panics) It's not here. I swear upon
the holy Bible, lord be my witness,
I don't have it.

                ED
(Returning from the John) What's the
problem now?

                JANE
He can't find his credit card. He
didn't bring it with him as usual.

                ED
Well, write a check.

                JANE
MARSHALL'S account is overdrawn because the doctor stopped payment on
his check until MARSHALL gives up red
meat.

                ED
All right. I'll pay. It's nothing new. I always
end up paying somehow with MARSHALL

                MARSHALL
ED, thank you. You saved me again.

                END

www.ingramcontent.com/pod-product-compliance
Lightning Source LLC
Chambersburg PA
CBHW021959160426
43197CB00007B/190